AF411944

Sarah's Midnight Anthology

Poems selected by Sarah Nock

A companion volume to
"Ponderings on Parkinson's"

Ferry House Books
www.ferryhousebooks.co.uk

Ferry House Books
Ferry House
Copthorne Bank
Copthorne
Crawley
West Sussex
RH10 3JF

www.ferryhousebooks.co.uk

This book is dedicated to

Louisa and Helen Nock

29th November 2005

PREFACE

Some years ago I actually had insomnia for a while. It surprised me for I had always found sleep the easiest of functions, indeed I did not really have it under control: sung evensong in a candlelit cathedral, a London double-decker, a jeep bouncing on jungle roads, a small aeroplane crossing the Atlantic with seats for only me and Peter – all induced almost instant sleep. Anyhow, I did what I could without disturbing Peter, who was not a contributor to such a nonsensical state. I recited to myself all the poems I knew by heart. Frustrated by the shortage of them, I would then put them into the "egg" language, or "backwords". But it wasn't the same; I yearned for other half-remembered but much loved poems. Then I was diagnosed with Parkinson's and found that in the last resort, when I felt absolutely foul and could do nothing for myself - when knitting, thinking, even crossword puzzles had been abandoned, then to be read poetry was a truly delicious distraction. As the dormouse who loved "geraniums red and delphiniums blue" would understand, it was the most "answering" thing I knew. The only trouble was that my dear readers would sometimes come up with poems I did not like, then all the angst returned. I had to protect myself somehow and thus I have gathered together a collection of poems that do not tire or bore me; that I have known for years and years (school days are more than half a century away) or ones that I have slipped easily into remembering -- because being with your reader, word by word, and recognising any mistake is part of the soothing effect. Thank you, dear readers: diffident friends, embarrassed grandchildren, wary contemporaries, all improving so much as they went along and actually, I do believe, beginning to like poetry. I do hope so, and that this will please them a little.

The picture on the front cover, taken by Pat Davidson

at their house, shortly after my PD diagnosis, is also important to me and part of the philosophical scene that poetry introduces. When I saw it, it all became clear to me: there I was, walking out of the picture! That was what was happening and that was what I had to prepare for. Mind you, I never expected so many years in which to prepare, and for that I can only thank my darling families and my very dear friends; it would not have been thus if they had been otherwise. So I am just going to quote Hilaire Belloc who says it all for me:

"From quiet homes and far beginning
Out to the undiscovered ends,
There's nothing worth the wear of winning
But laughter, and the love of friends".

Sarah Nock
May 26th 2008

ACKNOWLEDGEMENTS

Ferry House Books gratefully acknowledges the following personages and publishers for their assistance and most generous permission to reproduce copyright material:

Funeral Blues from *Collected Poems* by W H Auden, reproduced by permission of Faber and Faber Ltd.

Tarantella, Dedicatory Ode (Excerpt), Courtesy, Jim, by Hilaire Belloc (© Hilaire Belloc) is reproduced by permission of PFD on behalf of Hilaire Belloc.

Poems *Slough, A Subaltern's Love Song* and *Christmas,* from *Collected Poems*, by John Betjeman © 1955, 1958, 1962, 1964, 1968, 1970, 1979, 1981, 1982, 2001 Reproduced by permission of John Murray (Publishers).

To a Fat Lady seen from the Train by kind permission of the Trustees of the Mrs Frances C Cornford Deceased Will Trust.

Mama Dot by Fred D'Aguiar from *An English Sampler* by kind permission of Chatto and Windus.

Mr K P Griffin of Messrs Dee & Griffin, Trustee of Mrs H M Davies Will Trust, for permission to reproduce *Leisure* by W H Davies.

The Literary Trustees of Walter de la Mare and The Society of Authors as their representative for permission to reproduce *The Listeners, Poor Miss 7, Mistletoe* and *Sam* by Walter de la Mare.

Estate of the late James MacGibbon for *Not Waving but Drowning* by Stevie Smith.

Mr Gwydion Thomas for generous permission to use *Via Negativa* by his father, the late R.S. Thomas.

A P Watt Ltd on behalf of Gráinne Yeats for inclusion of *Down by the Salley Gardens, He Wishes for the Cloths of Heaven, Easter 1916, An Irish Airman Foresees his Death, The Song of Wandering Aengus, The Lake Isle of Innisfree, When You are Old* and *The Stolen Child* by W B Yeats.

We are grateful to the following for permission to include their poems: Sophie Aldrich for *The Lizard;* Mike Baddeley for *Farewell to a Colleague*; Sally Cade for *Lament, Advice* and *Declension;* Jennie Horsman for *Late Evening, Snowdrops, Shadowy Kings, Boy on the Gate* and *The Shepherd;* Peter Perrin for *Rejected Odyssey, The Familiar, Old Age, Dark to Dark,* and *A Faint Jingle from the Universe;* and Patricia Stott for *Yiddles.*

We are also very grateful for permission to use illustrations as follows:

Pat Davidson for allowing us to use her photograph of their garden (with Sarah Nock) and also for permission to reproduce her pastel drawing on page 53 as an illustration to *Trees* by Joyce Kilmer.

Edward Ardizzone for *Poor Miss 7, Mistletoe* and *Sam* from *Peacock Pie* by Walter de la Mare reprinted by kind

JOURNEY OF THE MAGI

A cold coming we had of it,
Just the worst time of the year
For a journey, and such a long journey:
The ways deep and the weather sharp,
The very dead of winter.
And the camels galled, sore-footed, refractory,
Lying down in the melting snow.
There were times we regretted
The summer palaces on slopes, the terraces,
And the silken girls bringing sherbet.

Then the camel men cursing and grumbling
And running away, and wanting their liquor and women,
And the night-fires going out, and the lack of shelters,
And the cities hostile and the towns unfriendly
And the villages dirty and charging high prices:
A hard time we had of it.
At the end we preferred to travel all night,
Sleeping in snatches,
With the voices singing in our ears, saying
That this was all folly.

Then at dawn we came down to a temperate valley,
Wet, below the snow line, smelling of vegetation,
With a running stream and a water-mill beating the darkness,
And three trees on the low sky.
And an old white horse galloping away in the meadow.
Then we came to a tavern with vine-leaves over the lintel,
Six hands at an open door dicing for pieces of silver,
And feet kicking the empty wine-skins.
But there was no information, so we continued
And arrived at evening, not a moment too soon
Finding the place: it was (you may say) satisfactory.

All this was a long time ago, I remember,
And I would do it again, but set down
This, set down
This: were we led all that way for
Birth or Death? There was a Birth, certainly,

With home-bred hordes the hillsides teem,
  The troop-ships bring us one by one,
At vast expense of time and steam,
  To slay Afridis where they run.
The "captives of our bow and spear"
Are cheap – alas! - as we are dear.

Rudyard Kipling
1865 - 1936

THE PASSING DAY, Excerpt

A late lark twitters from the quiet skies;
And from the west,
Where the sun, his day's work ended,
Lingers as in content,
There falls on the old, gray city
An influence luminous and serene,
A shining peace.

The smoke ascends
In a rosy-and-golden haze. The spires
Shine and are changed. In the valley
Shadows rise. The lark sings on. The sun,
Closing his benediction,
Sinks, and the darkening air
Thrills with a sense of the triumphing night—
Night with her train of stars
And her great gift of sleep.

So be my passing!
My task accomplish'd and the long day done,
My wages taken, and in my heart
Some late lark singing,
Let me be gather'd to the quiet West,
The sundown splendid and serene,
Death.

William Ernest Henley
1849 - 1903

ONE PERFECT ROSE

A single flow'r he sent me, since we met.
  All tenderly his messenger he chose;
Deep-hearted, pure, with scented dew still wet –
  One perfect rose.

I knew the language of the floweret;
  'My fragile leaves', it said 'his heart enclose'.
Love long has taken for his amulet
  One perfect rose.

Why is it no one ever sent me yet
  One perfect limousine, do you suppose?
Ah no, it's always just my luck to get
  One perfect rose.

Dorothy Parker
1893 - 1967

LINES FROM ENDYMION

A thing of beauty is a joy for ever:
Its loveliness increases; it will never
Pass into nothingness; but still will keep
A bower quiet for us, and a sleep
Full of sweet dreams, and health, and quiet breathing.
Therefore, on every morrow, are we wreathing
A flowery band to bind us to the earth,
Spite of despondence, of the inhuman dearth
Of noble natures, of the gloomy days,
Of all the unhealthy and o'er-darkened ways
Made for our searching: yes, in spite of all,
Some shape of beauty moves away the pall
From our dark spirits.

John Keats
1795 - 1821

ABOU BEN ADHEM

Abou Ben Adhem (may his tribe increase!)
Awoke one night from a deep dream of peace,
And saw, within the moonlight in his room,
Making it rich, and like a lily in bloom,
An angel writing in a book of gold:--
Exceeding peace had made Ben Adhem bold,
And to the presence in the room he said,
'What writest thou?" - The vision rais'd its head,
And with a look made of all sweet accord,
Answer'd, "The names of those who love the Lord.'
'And is mine one?" said Abou. "Nay, not so",
Replied the angel. Abou spoke more low,
But cheerly still; and said ,"I pray thee, then,
Write me as one that loves his fellow men."
The angel wrote, and vanish'd. The next night
It came again with a great wakening light,
And show'd the names whom love of God had blest,
And lo! Ben Adhem's name led all the rest.

Leigh Hunt
1784 - 1859

THE OLD VICARAGE, GRANTCHESTER, Excerpt
(Café des Westens, Berlin, May 1912)

Ah God! To see the branches stir
Across the moon at Grantchester!
To smell the thrilling-sweet and rotten,
Unforgettable, unforgotten
River-smell and hear the breeze
Sobbing in the little trees.
Say, do the elm-clumps greatly stand
Still guardians of that holy land?
The chestnut shade, in reverend dream,
The yet unacademic stream?
Is dawn a secret shy and cold
Anadyomene, silver-gold?
And sunset still a golden sea
From Haslingfield to Madingley?
And after, ere the night is born,
Do hares come out about the corn?
Oh, is the water sweet and cool,
Gentle and brown, above the pool?
And laughs the immortal river still
Under the mill, under the mill?
Say, is the Beauty yet to find?
And Certainty? and Quiet kind?
Deep meadows yet, for to forget
The lies, and truths, and pain? …oh! yet
Stands the Church clock at ten to three?
And is there honey still for tea?

Rupert Brooke
1887 - 1915

ALL MY DAYS

All my days
And half my nights
I search for you.
By candle lights,
By little streams,
By city wall
Where sparrows call.
In every wind,
In every mist,
I meet the lovers
You have kissed.
But only echoes do I find
Of longings you have left behind.

Half my nights,
And all my days,
In many
Half remembered ways
I search for you,
And long for you,
The one I'll tell my secrets to,
The lover I have loved before,
A thousand years. Or less…. Or more…
Your memory I keep in me,
Just half my nights, asleep in me –
And all my days, down deep in me.

Paxye Lucas
1918 - 2003

8

AS YOU LIKE IT, Excerpt
Act II Scene VII

Jaques:

All the world's a stage,
And all the men and women merely players:
They have their exits and their entrances;
And one man in his time plays many parts,
His acts being seven ages. As, first the infant,
Mewling and puking in the nurse's arms.
And then the whining school-boy, with his satchel,
And shining morning face, creeping like a snail
Unwillingly to school. And then the lover,
Sighing like furnace, with a woeful ballad
Made to his mistress' eyebrow. Then the soldier,
Full of strange oaths, and bearded like the pard,
Jealous in honour, sudden and quick in quarrel,
Seeking the bubble reputation
Even in the cannon's mouth. And then the justice,
In fair round belly with good capon lin'd,
With eyes severe, and beard of formal cut,
Full of wise saws and modern instances;
And so he plays his part. The sixth age shifts
Into the lean and slipper'd pantaloon,
With spectacles on nose and pouch on side;
His youthful hose well sav'd, a world too wide
For his shrunk shank; and his big manly voice,
Turning again toward childish treble, pipes
And whistles in his sound. Last scene of all,
That ends this strange eventful history,
Is second childishness and mere oblivion,
Sans teeth, sans eyes, sans taste, sans everything.

William Shakespeare
1564 - 1616

A SONG OF A YOUNG LADY TO HER ANCIENT LOVER

Ancient person, for whom I
All the flattering youth defy,
Long be it ere thou grow old,
Aching, shaking, crazy, cold;
But still continue as thou art,
Ancient person of my heart.

On thy withered lips and dry,
Which like barren furrows lie,
Brooding kisses I will pour
Shall thy youthful heat restore
(Such kind showers in autumn fall,
And a second spring recall);
Nor from thee will ever part,
Ancient person of my heart.

Thy nobler part, which but to name
In our sex would be counted shame,
By age's frozen grasp possessed,
From his ice shall be released,
And soothed by my reviving hand,
In former warmth and vigour stand.
All a lover's wish can reach
For thy joy my love shall teach,
And for thy pleasure shall improve
All that art can add to love.
Yet still I love thee without art,
Ancient person of my heart.

John Wilmot, Earl of Rochester
1647 - 1680

JERUSALEM, Excerpt

And did those feet in ancient time
Walk upon England's mountains green?
And was the holy lamb of God
On England's pleasant pastures seen?

And did the countenance divine
Shine forth upon our clouded hills?
And was Jerusalem builded here
Among those dark satanic mills?

Bring me my bow of burning gold;
Bring me my arrows of desire;
Bring me my spear; O clouds unfold!
Bring me my chariot of fire.

I will not cease from mental fight,
Nor shall my sword sleep in my hand
Till we have built Jerusalem
In England's green and pleasant land.

William Blake
1757 - 1827

HAMLET, Excerpt
Act I Scene III

Polonius to Laertes,

And these few precepts in thy memory
Look thou character. Give thy thoughts no tongue,
Nor any unproportion'd thought his act.
Be thou familiar, but by no means vulgar;
The friends thou hast, and their adoption tried,
Grapple them to thy soul with hoops of steel;
But do not dull thy palm with entertainment
Of each new-hatch'd, unfledg'd comrade. Beware
Of entrance to a quarrel; but, being in,

11

Bear't that th' opposed may beware of thee.
Give every man thine ear, but few thy voice;
Take each man's censure, but reserve thy judgment.
Costly thy habit as thy purse can buy,
But not express'd in fancy; rich, not gaudy;
For the apparel oft proclaims the man,
And they in France of the best rank and station
Are most select and generous, chief in that.
Neither a borrower, nor a lender be;
For loan oft loses both itself and friend,
And borrowing dulls the edge of husbandry,
This above all: to thine own self be true,
And it must follow, as the night the day,
Thou canst not then be false to any man.
Farewell; my blessing season this in thee!

William Shakespeare
1564 - 1616

AS KINGFISHERS CATCH FIRE

As kingfishers catch fire, dragonflies draw flame;
As tumbled over rim in roundy wells
Stones ring; like each tucked string tells, each hung bell's
Bow swung finds tongue to fling out broad its name;
Each mortal thing does one thing and the same:
Deals out that being indoors each one dwells;
Selves – goes itself; myself it speaks and spells,
Crying, What I do is me; for that I came.

I say more: the just man justices;
Keeps grace: that keeps all his goings graces;
Acts in God's eye what in God's eye he is—
Christ. For Christ plays in ten thousand places,
Lovely in limbs, and lovely in eyes not his
To the Father through the features of men's faces.

Gerard Manley Hopkins
1844 - 1889

12

THE RUBAIYAT OF OMAR KHAYYAM, Excerpt

(1)
Awake! for morning in the bowl of night
Has flung the stone that puts the stars to flight:
And lo! the hunter of the east has caught
The sultan's turret in a noose of light.

(11)
Here with a loaf of bread beneath the bough,
A flask of wine, a book of verse... and thou
Beside me singing in the wilderness...
And wilderness is paradise enow.

(16)
Think, in this battered caravanserai
Whose doorways are alternate night and day,
How sultan after sultan with his pomp
Abode his hour or two, and went his way.

(27)
Myself when young did eagerly frequent
Doctor and saint, and heard great argument
About it and about: but evermore
Came out by the same door as in I went.

(51)
The moving finger writes; and, having writ,
Moves on: nor all thy piety nor wit
Shall lure it back to cancel half a line,
Nor all thy tears wash out a word of it.

Edward FitzGerald
1809 - 1883

THE ROLLING ENGLISH ROAD

Before the Roman came to Rye or out to Severn strode,
The rolling English drunkard made the rolling English road.
A reeling road, a rolling road, that rambles round the shire,
And after him the parson ran, the sexton and the squire;
A merry road, a mazy road, and such as we did tread
The night we went to Birmingham by way of Beachy Head.

I knew no harm of Bonaparte and plenty of the Squire,
And for to fight the Frenchman I did not much desire;
But I did bash their baggonets because they came arrayed
To straighten out the crooked road an English drunkard made,
Where you and I went down the lane with ale-mugs in our
    hands,
The night we went to Glastonbury by way of Goodwin Sands.

His sins they were forgiven him; or why do flowers run
Behind him; and the hedges all strengthening in the sun?
The wild thing went from left to right and knew not which was
    which,
But the wild rose was above him when they found him in the
    ditch.
God pardon us, nor harden us; we did not see so clear
The night we went to Bannockburn by way of Brighton Pier.

My friends, we will not go again or ape an ancient rage,
Or stretch the folly of our youth to be the shame of age,
But walk with clearer eyes and ears this path that wandereth,
And see undrugged in evening light the decent inn of death;
For there is good news yet to hear and fine things to be seen,
Before we go to Paradise by way of Kensal Green.

G.K. Chesterton
1874 - 1936

LATE EVENING

Beneath arched arms of shaded trees
Late evening hangs its dusky veils
And Summer breathes across warmed walls
Where ivy runs its darkened trails.

Abroad from barns and ageing tiles
Bats weave a fast elastic flight,
They flaunt their fancy trickery
Beyond a screen of steely light

As fading soft sleeved boughs unite
And roosting birds in eves confide,
Last faint searching squeaks are heard
Then bats and night collide.

Jennie Horsman
1937 -

MAMA DOT

Born on a sunday
In the kingdom of Ashante

Sold on monday
Into slavery

Ran away on tuesday
Cause she born free

Lost a foot on wednesday
When they catch she

Worked all thursday
Till her head grey

Dropped on friday
Where they burned she

Freed on saturday
In a new century

Fred D'aguiar
1960 -

BREAK, BREAK, BREAK

Break, break, break,
  On thy cold grey stones, O Sea!
And I would that my tongue could utter
  The thoughts that arise in me.

O well for the fisherman's boy,
  That he shouts with his sister at play!
O well for the sailor lad,
  That he sings in his boat on the bay!

And the stately ships go on
  To their haven under the hill;
But O for the touch of a vanished hand,
  And the sound of a voice that is still!

Break, break, break,
  At the foot of thy crags, O Sea!
But the tender grace of a day that is dead
  Will never come back to me.

Alfred, Lord Tennyson
1809 - 1892

REJECTED ODYSSEY

Can you not now remember
How we felt the limbs of the Downland
Stretching to rest
Under the green turf
With the chalk white revelation of her breast
Through the blown garment of the grass?
Until in a dewpond
Night flashed a smile in an instant's reflection,
And we comprehended the intense face of beauty.
But you were afraid,
Self clipped your wings
To find reassurance in people
And the dross of habitual things.

I wanted you to turn
And sail outwards with me
To a world I could not conquer alone
Save you stretched hands
To the ropes of my argosy.

We would have seen the shares of day
Ploughing the blue arable of darkness,
The sun flowering in those bright furrows
Unfolding and thrusting its pollen heart
To the high noon.

But the wine of a dying world
Runs purple and red in the beechwoods
Earth curls her wintry lips to the falling treasuries
Leaf on leaf rustling and nestling to silence on her cheek.

The boulders of the clouds
Are rolling to their disintegration
In the splinters of the rain.
Fields lifting invisible mouths
Thirst, and are assuaged at the drench.

Why have you deserted these cities of earth and air
For the man-built huddles of security?
Were the cloisters of evening not sufficient
For your contemplation,
Or the fountains of morning for your ecstasy?

Peter Perrin
1917 -

GOOD AND BAD CHILDREN

Children, you are very little,
And your bones are very brittle;
If you would grow great and stately,
You must try to walk sedately.

You must still be bright and quiet,
And content with simple diet;
And remain, through all bewild'ring
Innocent and honest children.

Happy hearts and happy faces,
Happy play in grassy places -
That was how, in ancient ages,
Children grew to kings and sages.

But the unkind and the unruly,
And the sort who eat unduly,
They must never hope for glory -
Theirs is quite a different story!

Cruel children, crying babies,
All grow up as geese and gabies,
Hated, as their age increases,
 By their nephews and their nieces.

Robert Louis Stevenson
1850 - 1894

THE FORSAKEN MERMAN

Come, dear children let us away;
Down and away below.
Now my brothers call from the bay;
Now the great winds shorewards blow,
Now the salt tides seawards flow;
Now the wild white horses play,
Champ and chafe and toss in the spray.
Children dear, let us away
This way, this way.

Call her once before you go.
Call once yet
In a voice that she will know:
"Margaret! Margaret!"
Children's voices should be dear
(Call once more) to a mother's ear:
Children's voices wild with pain,
Surely she will come again?
Call her once and come away

This way, this way.
"Mother dear, we cannot stay."
The wild white horses foam and fret.
Margaret! Margaret!

Come, dear children, come away down.
Call no more.
One last look at the white-wall'd town,
And the little grey church on the windy shore,
Then come down.
She will not come though you call all day.
Come away, come away.

Children dear, was it yesterday
We heard the sweet bells over the bay?
In the caverns where we lay,
Through the surf and through the swell
The far-off sound of a silver bell?
Sand-strewn caverns, cool and deep,
Where the winds are all asleep;
Where the spent lights quiver and gleam;
Where the salt weed sways in the stream;
Where the sea-beasts ranged all round
Feed in the ooze of their pasture-ground;
Where the sea-snakes coil and twine,
Dry their mail and bask in the brine;
Where great whales come sailing by,
Sail and sail with unshut eye,
Round the world for ever and aye?
When did the music come this way?
Children dear, was it yesterday?

Children dear, was it yesterday
(Call yet once) that she went away?
Once she sate with you and me,
On a red gold throne in the heart of the sea,
And the youngest sate on her knee.
She comb'd its bright hair, and she tended it well,
When down swung the sound of a far-off bell.
She looked up through the clear green sea,
She said: "I must go, for my kinsfolk pray

In the little grey church on the shore today.
'Twill be Easter-time in the world – ah me!
And I lose my poor soul, Merman, here with thee."
I said: 'Go up, dear heart, through the waves;
Say thy prayer, and come back to the kind sea-caves!'
She smiled, she went up through the surf in the bay.
Children dear, was it yesterday.

Children dear, were we long alone?
The sea grows stormy, the little ones moan.
"Long prayers", I said, "in the world they say;
Come," I said, and we rose through the surf in the bay,
We went up the beach, by the sandy down
Where the sea-stocks bloom, to the white-wall'd town.
Through the narrow pav'd streets, where all was still,
To the little grey church on the windy hill.
From the church came a murmur of folk at their prayers,
But we stood without in the cold blowing airs.
We climb'd on the graves, on the stones, worn with rains,
And we gaz'd up the aisle through the small leaded panes.
She sat by the pillar; we saw her clear;
"Margaret, hist! Come quick, we are here.
Dear heart", I said, "we are long alone;
The sea grows stormy, the little ones moan."
But, ah, she gave me never a look,
For her eyes were seal'd to the holy book.
Loud prays the priest; shut stands the door.
Come away, children, call no more.
Come away, come down, call no more.

Down, down, down.
Down to the depths of the sea.
She sits at her wheel in the humming town,
Singing most joyfully,
Hark what she sings: "O joy, O joy,
For the humming street, and the child with its toy,
For the priest, and the bell, and the holy well.
For the wheel where I spun,
And the blessed light of the sun."
And so she sings her fill.
Singing most joyfully,

Till the shuttle falls from her hand,
And the whizzing wheel stands still.
She steals to the window and looks at the sand;
And over the sand at the sea;
And her eyes are set in a stare;
And anon there breaks a sigh,
And anon there drops a tear,
From a sorry-clouded eye,
And a heart sorrow-laden,
A long, long sigh.
For the cold, strange eyes of a little Mermaiden
And the gleam of her golden hair.

Come away, away children.
Come children, come down.
The hoarse wind blows colder;
Lights shine in the town.
She will start from her slumber
When gusts shake the door;
She will hear the winds howling,
Will hear the waves roar.
We shall see, while above us
The waves roar and whirl,
A ceiling of amber,
A pavement of pearl.
Singing: "Here came a mortal,
But faithless was she,
And alone dwell for ever
The kings of the sea."
But, children, at midnight,
When soft the winds blow:
When clear falls the moonlight;
When spring-tides are low;
When sweet airs come seaward
From heaths starr'd with broom;
And high rocks throw mildly
On the blanch'd sands a gloom;
Up the still, glistening beaches,
Up the creeks we will hie;
Over banks of bright seaweed
The ebb-tide leaves dry.

We will gaze, from the sand-hills,
At the white, sleeping town;
At the church on the hillside—
And then come back down.
Singing: "There dwells a lov'd one,
But cruel is she.
She left lonely for ever
The kings of the sea."

Matthew Arnold
1822 - 1888

SLOUGH

Come, friendly bombs, and fall on Slough
It isn't fit for humans now,
There isn't grass to graze a cow
  Swarm over, Death!

Come, bombs, and blow to smithereens
Those air-conditioned, bright canteens
Tinned fruit, tinned meat, tinned milk, tinned beans
  Tinned minds, tinned breath.

Mess up the mess they call a town--
A house for ninety-seven down
And once a week a half-a-crown
  For twenty years,

And get that man with double chin
Who'll always cheat and always win,
Who washes his repulsive skin
  In women's tears,

And smash his desk of polished oak
And smash his hands so used to stroke
And stop his boring dirty joke
  And make him yell.

But spare the bald young clerks who add
The profits of the stinking cad;
It's not their fault that they are mad,
  They've tasted Hell.

It's not their fault they do not know
The birdsong from the radio,
It's not their fault they often go
  To Maidenhead.

And talk of sports and makes of cars
In various bogus Tudor bars
And daren't look up and see the stars
  But belch instead.

In labour-saving homes, with care
Their wives frizz out peroxide hair
And dry it in synthetic air
  And paint their nails.

Come friendly bombs, and fall on Slough
To get it ready for the plough.
The cabbages are coming now;
  The earth exhales

John Betjeman
1906 - 1984

SNOWDROPS

Come ladies shivering there
Beneath frost wrapped trees,
Feel my hand it is warm.
I will take you to a place
Where you, in your scant
White attire, will not shiver.

Though your elegance
And bold tenacity endure,
I fear for your beauty.
The wild wind stings
Scarring breath upon you
In unceasing assault.

Now in the room's warmth
See the mirror's image
As you rest in a cradle of glass
Bathed in watery wealth
Yet you display
No sign of gratitude

You fade so fast;
You are wizened so soon
And no longer lissome
As those aquiver outside
Where Winter's bleak crust
Bears their fragile allure.

Jennie Horsman
1937 -

SONNET FOR THE MADONNA OF THE CHERRIES

Dear Lady of the Cherries, cool, serene,
Untroubled by our follies, strife and fears,
Clad in soft reds and blues and mantle green,
Your memory has been with me all these years.

Long years of battle, bitterness and waste,
Dry years of sun and dust and Eastern skies,
Hard years of ceaseless struggle, endless haste,
Fighting 'gainst greed for power and hate and lies.

Your red-gold hair, your slowly smiling face
For pride in your dear son, your King of Kings,
Fruits of the kindly earth, and truth and grace,
Colour and light, and all warm lovely things-

For all that loveliness, that warmth, that light,
Blessed Madonna, I go back to fight.

Lord Wavell
1883 - 1950

LAMENT

Death came to our house as a friend;
Was not announced at the front door;
Not barked at;
We sat him down and offered tea.

Jones, he said his name was,
He could as well have told us Smith for all we cared-
And so it was not true we held him as a friend
But we were courteous in disinterest.

He sat there, smiling slyly
And watched us being busy and preoccupied.
We never asked him where he lived nor where he came from,
No one saw him go-- he left us as a thief,
Taking the very heart of us away.

Bar the door, lock the windows!
If any come, ask his business.
Demand to see credentials, be suspicious, urgent.
Let no man come within who cannot be accounted for.

Yet he will come, he always has,
Tradition is upon his side,
No family love, no desperate need, has yet withstood him;
He will take that which he came for.

But had we known, when Death came to our house as a
friend,
Had we known his business or cared enough to ask him more-
Then when he went,
At least we could have said "Goodbye".

Sally Cade
1935 -

No sound
In the walls of the Halls where falls
The tread
Of the feet of the dead to the ground.
No sound:
But the boom
Of the far Waterfall like Doom.

Hilaire Belloc
1870 - 1953

UP-HILL

Does the road wind uphill all the way?
  Yes, to the very end.
Will the day's journey take the whole long day?
  From morn to night, my friend.

But is there for the night a resting-place?
  A roof for when the slow dark hours begin.
May not the darkness hide it from my face?
  You cannot miss that inn.

Shall I meet other wayfarers at night?
  Those who have gone before.
Then must I knock, or call when just in sight?
  They will not keep you waiting at that door.

Shall I find comfort, travel-sore and weak?
  Of labour you shall find the sum.
Will there be beds for me and all who seek?
  Yea, beds for all who come.

Christina Rossetti
1830 - 1894

DOWN BY THE SALLEY GARDENS

Down by the salley gardens my love and I did meet;
She passed the salley gardens with little snow-white feet.
She bid me take love easy, as the leaves grow on the tree;
But I, being young and foolish, with her would not agree.

In a field by the river my love and I did stand,
And on my leaning shoulder she laid her snow-white hand.
She bid me take life easy, as the grass grows on the weirs;
But I was young and foolish, and now am full of tears.

W.B. Yeats
1865 - 1939

COMPOSED UPON WESTMINSTER BRIDGE
September 3, 1802

Earth has not anything to show more fair;
Dull would he be of soul who could pass by
A sight so touching in its majesty:
This city now doth, like a garment, wear
The beauty of the morning; silent, bare,
Ships, towers, domes, theatres, and temples lie
Open unto the fields, and to the sky,
All bright and glittering in the smokeless air.
Never did sun more beautifully steep
In his first splendour, valley, rock, or hill;
Ne'er saw I, never felt, a calm so deep!
The river glideth at his own sweet will:
Dear God! The very houses seem asleep;
And all that mighty heart is lying still!

William Wordsworth
1770 - 1850

EVERYONE SANG

Every one suddenly burst out singing;
And I was filled with such delight
As prisoned birds must find in freedom
Winging wildly across the white
Orchards and dark green fields; on; on; and out of sight.

Every one's voice was suddenly lifted,
And beauty came like the setting sun.
My heart was shaken with tears, and horror
Drifted away ..... O, but every one
Was a bird; and the song was wordless; the singing will
          never be done.

Siegfried Sassoon
1886 - 1967

FIRST THEY CAME FOR THE JEWS

First they came for the Jews
and I did not speak out –
because I was not a Jew.
Then they came for the communists
and I did not speak out –
because I was not a communist.
Then they came for the trade unionists
and I did not speak out –
because I was not a trade unionist.
Then they came for me –
and there was no one left
to speak out for me.

Pastor Niemoller
1892 – 1984

THE LIZARD

Flits in and out of tiny speckled stones
Scuttles like a spider
Sliding up the palm tree on a shady branch
Coconuts sway in the wind, rattling together like castanets
Tail quivers, feet like suction pads
Tongue forked like a match flame, flickers
Plucks at hovering mosquitoes
A born gymnast
Life like a dance routine
Turning flips
Flimsy skeleton like a pencil lead, snappable
Light body; so light the wind could carry this creature
And throw it onto the shingly beach.

The lizard basks in the scorching sun
He writhes and darts down the tread bark
Tracks unnoticed
Like a gypsy, it has no home
Always on the move, exploring new places
Bold and unflinching
Escaping every trouble
Hiding under dry rocks
Smiling slyly.

Sophie Aldrich (aged 10)
1994 -

A MEMORY

Four ducks on a pond,
A grass-bank beyond,
A blue sky of spring,
White clouds on the wing:
What a little thing
To remember for years--
To remember with tears!

William Allingham
1828 - 1889

DEDICATORY ODE, Excerpt

From quiet homes and first beginning,
Out to the undiscovered ends,
There's nothing worth the wear of winning,
But laughter and the love of friends.

Hilaire Belloc
1870 - 1953

ADVICE

Get on with being yourself, man.
Don't look sideways – you might see something you don't like.
Purchase for yourself the best of everything you can.
Don't look sideways, you might see another human being.

The good things in life are there for you, man.
Hi-fi, stereos, digital watches.
Your poor old aunt died yesterday.   Buy yourself a new shirt,
Don't you get involved, man – it leads to stomach ache.

Forget the way the digital years roll by;
That age will have its fling with you.
Turn the hi-fi louder, put the earphones on -
Don't let the loneliness sneak in.

Sally Cade
1935 -

HE WISHES FOR THE CLOTHS OF HEAVEN

Had I the heavens' embroidered cloths,
Enwrought with golden and silver light,
The blue and the dim and the dark cloths
Of night and light and the half-light,
I would spread the cloths under your feet:
But I, being poor, have only my dreams;
I have spread my dreams under your feet;
Tread softly because you tread on my dreams.

William Butler Yeats
1865 - 1939

TO HIS COY MISTRESS

Had we but world enough, and time,
This coyness, Lady, were no crime,
We would sit down, and think which way
To walk, and pass our long love's day.
Thou by the Indian Ganges' side
Shouldst rubies find: I by the tide
Of Humber would complain. I would
Love you ten years before the flood,
And you should, if you please, refuse
Till the conversion of the Jews;
My vegetable love should grow
Vaster than empires and more slow;
An hundred years should go to praise
Thine eyes, and on thy forehead gaze;
Two hundred to adore each breast,
But thirty thousand to the rest;
An age at least to every part,
And the last age should show your heart.
For, Lady, you deserve this state,
Nor would I love at lower rate.
But at my back I always hear
Time's winged chariot hurrying near,
And yonder all before us lie
Deserts of vast eternity . . .
Thy beauty shall no more be found,
Nor, in thy marble vault, shall sound
My echoing song: then worms shall try
That long preserved virginity,
And your quaint honour turn to dust,
And into ashes all my lust:
The grave's a fine and private place
But none, I think, do there embrace.
Now, therefore, while the youthful hue
Sits on thy skin like morning dew,
And while thy willing soul transpires
At every pore with instant fires,
Now let us sport us while we may;
And now, like amorous birds of prey,
Rather at once our time devour,

Than languish in his slow-chapp'd power.
Let us roll all our strength and all
Our sweetness up into one ball,
And tear our pleasures with rough strife
Thorough the iron gates of life.
Thus, though we cannot make our Sun
Stand still, yet we will make him run.

Andrew Marvell
1621 - 1678

SOLITUDE

Happy the man, whose wish and care
A few paternal acres bound,
Content to breathe his native air
  In his own ground.

Whose herds with milk, whose fields with bread,
Whose flocks supply him with attire;
Whose trees in summer yield him shade,
  In winter fire.

Blest, who can unconcernedly find
Hours, days and years, slide soft away
In health of body, peace of mind,
  Quiet by day.

Sound sleep by night; study and ease
Together mixed; sweet recreation,
And innocence, which most does please
  With meditation.

Thus let me live, unseen, unknown;
Thus unlamented let me die;
Steal from the world, and not a stone
  Tell where I lie.

Alexander Pope
1688 - 1744

TO GOD XVII, Excerpt

He who bends to himself a Joy
Doth the winged life destroy;
But he who kisses the Joy as it flies
Lives in Eternity's sunrise.

William Blake
1757 - 1827

HOW DO I LOVE THEE? LET ME COUNT THE WAYS

How do I love thee? Let me count the ways.
I love thee to the depth and breadth and height
My soul can reach, when feeling out of sight
For the ends of Being and ideal Grace.
I love thee to the level of every day's
Most quiet need, by sun and candlelight.
I love thee freely, as men strive for Right;
I love thee purely, as they turn from Praise.
I love thee with the passion put to use
In my old griefs, and with my childhood's faith.
I love thee with a love I seemed to lose
With my lost saints,- I love thee with the breath,
Smiles, tears, of all my life! - and, if God choose,
I shall but love thee better after death.

Elizabeth Barrett Browning
1806 - 1861

THE FAMILIAR

How long have I known you?
I have known you for the all of my life.
Where are you?
You are everywhere.
You are not only the ashes of life
Stored neatly on a shelf in Golders Green,
The slit corpse appraised by students or Michelangelo,
The marionettes crumpled in metal on the highways.
I have known you
In the stiff sleep of a collie
Never more to dream of scattered sheep on the blustery fell.
In the great oaks prostrate
Their beseeching arms twisted and broken in the hurricane.
I have heard you whimper and scream thinly to me
From the woods at night,
The faint cries of unknown calamities.
You are as voracious on the tidy lawn
As in the vast plains of the Serengeti.
On scuttering creatures
I have seen you stoop with folded wings
From the blue firmament where the skylark sings,
I think you know where the swallows are
That never came that Summer
To the mud nest empty in the shadow of the eaves.
You send the monstrous ships
To suck the frantic, living silver from the deeps,
The harpooned whale knows you
Cradled in the sanguine sea.
More cryptic, you are lurking in the caesium of the reindeer
moss,
Or in the genes of life itself
Disguised in the hidden spirals of creation.
You have looked at me coldly
You have diminished me
Through the eyes of she who once beheld me with love
When I was young and it mattered.
You were beside me when the picture painted, the words
written

Were abandoned as too ordinary,
Or hope forsook me in truth too hard to bear.
You are kind to some
Who do not know you when you come.
But how terrible for those who see
Your slow approach in all your dark and awesome panoply.
Then sometimes quietly you appear
Apparelled in your Autumn gold and red
But soon such dazzling garments shed
To howl upon the Winter winds
Or triumph in the snow
Over the brittled, naked earth below.
But then impatient you can take
The children, like Pied Piper
On your dreadful dance,
Not waiting for the passing year…
How long have I known you?
I have known you for the all of my life
Nor will it be long now
Nor of my choosing
When face to face
We shall meet for the last time
And I shall be in your embrace
Insentient
Oh Death,
Forever.

Peter Perrin
1917 -

DIRGE WITHOUT MUSIC

I am not resigned to the shutting away of loving hearts in the
hard ground.
So it is, and so it will be, for so it has been, time out of mind:
Into the darkness they go, the wise and the lovely. Crowned
With lilies and with laurel they go; but I am not resigned.

Lovers and thinkers, into the earth with you.
Be one with the dull, the indiscriminate dust.
A fragment of what you felt, of what you knew,
A formula, a phrase remains,--but the best is lost.

The answers quick and keen, the honest look, the laughter,
the love,
They are gone. They are gone to feed the roses. Elegant and
curled
Is the blossom. Fragrant is the blossom. I know. But I do not
approve.
More precious was the light in your eyes than all the roses in
the world.

Down, down, down into the darkness of the grave
Gently they go, the beautiful, the tender, the kind;
Quietly they go, the intelligent, the witty, the brave.
I know. But I do not approve. And I am not resigned.

Edna St. Vincent Millay
1892 - 1950

A POET'S LAST THOUGHTS
(WRITTEN IN NORTHAMPTON COUNTY ASYLUM)

I am! yet what I am who cares, or knows?
   My friends forsake me like a memory lost
I am the self-consumer of my woes;
   They rise and vanish, an oblivious host,
Shadows of life, whose very soul is lost.
And yet I am - I live - though I am toss'd

Into the nothingness of scorn and noise,
   Into the living sea of waking dream,
Where there is neither sense of life, nor joys,
   But the huge shipwreck of my own esteem
And all that's dear. Even those I loved the best
Are strange – nay, they are stranger than the rest.

I long for scenes where man has never trod –
   For scenes where woman never smiled or wept –
There to abide with my Creator, God,
   And sleep as I in childhood sweetly slept,
Full of high thoughts, unborn. So let me lie –
The grass below; above, the vaulted sky.

John Clare
1793 - 1864

SONNET 41

I, being born a woman and distressed
By all the needs and notions of my kind,
Am urged by your propinquity to find
Your person fair, and feel a certain zest
To bear your body's weight upon my breast;
So subtly is the fume of life designed,
To clarify the pulse and cloud the mind,

And leave me once again undone, possessed.
Think not for this, however, the poor treason
Of my stout blood against my staggering brain,
I shall remember you with love, or season
My scorn with pity, - let me make it plain:
I find this frenzy insufficient reason
For conversation when we meet again.

Edna St Vincent Millay
1892 - 1950

I EXPECT

I expect to pass through this world but once; any good thing
therefore that I can do, or any kindness that I can show to any
fellow-creature, let me do it now; let me not defer or neglect it,
for I shall not pass this way again.

Attr. Stephen Grellet
1773 - 1855

HEAVEN-HAVEN
A NUN TAKES THE VEIL

I have desired to go
Where springs not fail,
To fields where flies no sharp and sided hail
And a few lilies blow.

And I have asked to be
Where no storms come,
Where the green swell is in the havens dumb,
And out of the swing of the sea.

Gerard Manley Hopkins
1844 - 1889

EASTER, 1916

I have met them at the close of day
Coming with vivid faces
From counter or desk among grey
Eighteenth-century houses.
I have passed with a nod of the head
Or polite meaningless words,
Or have lingered awhile and said
Polite meaningless words,
And thought before I had done
Of a mocking tale or a gibe
To please a companion
Around the fire at the club,
Being certain that they and I
But lived where motley is worn:
All changed, changed utterly:
A terrible beauty is born.

That woman's days were spent
In ignorant good-will,
Her nights in argument
Until her voice grew shrill.
What voice more sweet than hers
When young and beautiful,
She rode to harriers?
This man had kept a school
And rode our winged horse;
He might have won fame in the end,
So sensitive his nature seemed,
So daring and sweet his thought.
This other man I had dreamed
A drunken, vain-glorious lout.
He had done most bitter wrong
To some who are near my heart,
Yet I number him in the song;
He, too, has resigned his part
In the casual comedy;

He, too, has been changed in his turn,
Transformed utterly:
A terrible beauty is born.

Hearts with one purpose alone
Through summer and winter seem
Enchanted to a stone
To trouble the living stream.
The horse that comes from the road,
The rider, the birds that range
From cloud to tumbling cloud,
Minute by minute they change;
A shadow of cloud on the stream
Changes minute by minute;
A horse-hoof slides on the brim,
And a horse plashes within it;
The long-legged moor-hens call;
Minute by minute they live:
The stone's in the midst of all.

Too long a sacrifice
Can make a stone of the heart.
O when may it suffice?
That is Heaven's part, our part
To murmur name upon name,
As a mother names her child
When sleep at last has come
On limbs that had run wild.
What is it but nightfall?
No, no, not night but death;
Was it needless death after all?
For England may keep faith
For all that is done and said.
We know their dream; enough
To know they dreamed and are dead;
And what if excess of love
Bewildered them till they died?
I write it out in a verse--
MacDonagh and MacBride
And Connolly and Pearse

Now and in time to be,
Wherever green is worn,
Are changed, changed utterly:
A terrible beauty is born.

W. B. Yeats
1865 - 1939

THE WHITE CLIFFS, Excerpt

I have seen much to hate here – much to forgive,
But in a world where England is finished and dead
I do not wish to live.

Alice Duer Miller
1874 - 1942

THE OLD SHIPS

I have seen old ships sail like swans asleep
Beyond the village which men still call Tyre,
With leaden age o'er cargoed, dipping deep
For Famagusta and the hidden sun
That rings black Cyprus with a lake of fire;
And all those ships were certainly so old
Who knows how oft with squat and noisy gun,
Questing brown slaves or Syrian oranges,
The pirate Genoese
Hell-raked them till they rolled
Blood, water, fruit and corpses up the hold.
But now through friendly seas they softly run,
Painted the mid-sea blue or shore-sea green,
Still patterned with the vine and grapes in gold.

But I have seen,
Pointing her shapely shadows from the dawn
An image tumbled on a rose-swept bay,
A drowsy ship of some yet older day;
And, wonder's breath indrawn,
Thought I – who knows – who knows – but in that same
(Fished up beyond Æææa, patched up new
- Stern painted brighter blue -)
That talkative bald-headed seaman came
(Twelve patient comrades sweating at the oar)
From Troy's doom-crimson shore,
And with great lies about his wooden horse
Set the crew laughing, and forgot his course.

It was so old a ship – who knows – who knows?
And yet so beautiful, I watched in vain
To see the mast burst open with a rose,
And the whole deck put on its leaves again.

James Elroy Flecker
1884 - 1915

AN IRISH AIRMAN FORESEES HIS DEATH

I know that I shall meet my fate
    Somewhere among the clouds above;
Those that I fight I do not hate,
    Those that I guard I do not love;
My country is Kiltartan Cross,
    My countrymen Kiltartan's poor,
No likely end could bring them loss
    Or leave them happier than before.

Nor law, nor duty bade me fight,
    Nor public men, nor cheering crowds,
A lonely impulse of delight

Drove to this tumult in the clouds;
I balanced all, brought all to mind,
    The years to come seemed waste of breath,
A waste of breath the years behind
    In balance with this life, this death.

William Butler Yeats
1865 - 1939

JULIUS CAESAR, Excerpt
Act I, Scene III

Cassius:

I know where I will wear this dagger, then;
Cassius from bondage will deliver Cassius:
Therein, ye gods, you make the weak most
    strong;
Therein, ye gods, you tyrants do defeat:
Nor stony tower, nor walls of beaten brass,
Nor airless dungeon, nor strong links of iron,
Can be retentive to the strength of spirit:
But life, being weary of these worldly bars,
Never lacks power to dismiss itself.
If I know this, know all the world besides,
That part of tyranny that I do bear
I can shake off at pleasure.

William Shakespeare
1564 - 1616

THE DARKLING THRUSH

I leaned upon a coppice gate
  When Frost was spectre-gray,
And Winter's dregs made desolate
  The weakening eye of day.
The tangled bine-stems scored the sky
  Like strings of broken lyres,
And all mankind that haunted nigh
  Had sought their household fires.

The land's sharp features seemed to be
  The Century's corpse outleant,
His crypt the cloudy canopy,
  The wind his death-lament.
The ancient pulse of germ and birth
  Was shrunken hard and dry,
And every spirit upon earth
  Seem'd fervourless as I.

At once a voice arose among
  The bleak twigs overhead
In a full-hearted evensong
  Of joy illimited;
An aged thrush, frail, gaunt, and small,
  In blast-beruffled plume,
Had chosen thus to fling his soul
  Upon the growing gloom.

So little cause for carollings
  Of such ecstatic sound
Was written on terrestrial things
  Afar or nigh around,
That I could think there trembled through
  His happy good-night air
Some bless'd Hope, whereof he knew
  And I was unaware.

Thomas Hardy
1840 - 1928

OUT OF SYNC

I looked for you in Regent's Park,
I looked for you in far Bangkok.
I looked and looked beneath each tree
And waited under every clock.
But never we met – you'd always gone,
Though something of you lingered on.

I searched for you in crooked streets,
And where the Blue Nile starts its day.
By the roaring Tissisat waterfalls
I hoped you'd be there, drenched in spray.
But never we met – your path and mine
Would criss-cross out of sync with time.

In Afghanistan – yes I've been there too
In a dusty car to search for you –
Where the camels pass, at each mud serai,
And where the minarettes pierce the sky
I would look and look, then sadly say
"Perhaps tomorrow if not today...."

We've met before. I know you well.
I can't remember how or when.
A thousand years can spatter by
Before a chance to meet again.
But one bright day – why there you'll be!
The glow that lights my Christmas tree.
The longing other half of me!

Paxye Lucas
1918 - 2003

ALL BEAUTEOUS THINGS

I love all beauteous things,
   I seek and adore them;
God hath no better praise,
And man in his hasty days
   Is honoured for them.

I too will something make
   And joy in the making;
Although to-morrow it seem
Like empty words of a dream
   Remembered on waking.

Robert Bridges
1844 - 1930

OZYMANDIAS

I met a traveller from an antique land
Who said: Two vast and trunkless legs of stone
Stand in the desert. Near them, on the sand,
Half sunk, a shattered visage lies, whose frown,
And wrinkled lip, and sneer of cold command,
Tell that its sculptor well those passions read
Which yet survive, stamped on these lifeless things,
The hand that mocked them, and the heart that fed:
And on the pedestal these words appear:
'My name is Ozymandias, king of kings:
Look on my works, ye Mighty, and despair!'
Nothing beside remains. Round the decay
Of that colossal wreck, boundless and bare
The lone and level sands stretch far away.

Percy Bysshe Shelley
1792 - 1822

SEA FEVER

I must go down to the seas again, to the lonely sea and the
                sky,
And all I ask is a tall ship and a star to steer her by,
And the wheel's kick and the wind's song and the white sail's
                shaking,
And a grey mist on the sea's face, and a grey dawn breaking.

I must go down to the seas again, for the call of the running
                tide
Is a wild call and a clear call that may not be denied;
And all I ask is a windy day with the white clouds flying,
And the flung spray and the blown spume, and the sea-gulls
                crying.

I must go down to the seas again, to the vagrant gypsy life,
To the gull's way and the whale's way where the wind's like a
                whetted knife;
And all I ask is a merry yarn from a laughing fellow-rover,
And quiet sleep and a sweet dream when the long trick's over.

John Masefield
1878 - 1967

TREES

I think that I shall never see
A poem lovely as a tree

A tree whose hungry mouth is pressed
Against the earth's sweet flowing breast

A tree that looks at God all day
And lifts her leafy arms to pray

A tree that may in summer wear
A nest of robins in her hair

Upon whose bosom snow has lain
Who intimately lives with rain

Poems are made by fools like me
But only God can make a tree.

Joyce Kilmer
1888 - 1918

AN ANCIENT GESTURE

I thought, as I wiped my eyes on the corner of my apron:
Penelope did this too.
And more than once: you can't keep weaving all day
And undoing it all through the night;
Your arms get tired, and the back of your neck gets tight;
And along towards morning, when you think it will never be
        light,
And your husband has been gone, and you don't know where,
        for years,
Suddenly you burst into tears;
There is simply nothing else to do.

And I thought, as I wiped my eyes on the corner of my apron:
This is an ancient gesture, authentic, antique,
In the very best tradition, classic, Greek;
Ulysses did this too.
But only as a gesture, -- a gesture which implied
To the assembled throng that he was much too moved to
        speak.
He learned it from Penelope...
Penelope, who really cried.

Edna St Vincent Millay
1892 - 1950

THE SONG OF WANDERING AENGUS

I went out to the hazel wood,
    Because a fire was in my head,
And cut and peeled a hazel wand,
    And hooked a berry to a thread;
And when white moths were on the wing,
    And moth-like stars were flickering out,
I dropped the berry in a stream
    And caught a little silver trout.

When I had laid it on the floor
    I went to blow the fire aflame,
But something rustled on the floor,
    And some one called me by my name:
It had become a glimmering girl
    With apple blossom in her hair
Who called me by name and ran
    And faded through the brightening air.

Though I am old with wandering
    Through hollow lands and hilly lands,
I will find out where she has gone,
    And kiss her lips and take her hands;
And walk among long dappled grass,
    And pluck till time and times are done
The silver apples of the moon,
    The golden apples of the sun.

William Butler Yeats
1865 - 1939

THE LAKE ISLE OF INNISFREE

I will arise and go now, and go to Innisfree,
And a small cabin build there, of clay and wattles made;
Nine bean rows will I have there, a hive for the honeybee,
And live alone in the bee-loud glade.

And I shall have some peace there, for peace comes dropping
                                                        slow,
Dropping from the veils of the morning to where the cricket
                                                        sings;
There midnight's all a glimmer, and noon a purple glow,
And evening full of the linnet's wings.

I will arise and go now, for always night and day
I hear lake water lapping with low sounds by the shore;
While I stand on the roadway, or on the pavements grey,
I hear it in the deep heart's core.

William Butler Yeats
1865 - 1939

THE SOLDIER

If I should die, think only this of me:
  That there's some corner of a foreign field
That is for ever England. There shall be
  In that rich earth a richer dust concealed;
A dust whom England bore, shaped, made aware,
  Gave, once, her flowers to love, her ways to roam,
A body of England's, breathing English air,
  Washed by the rivers, blest by suns of home.

And think, this heart, all evil shed away,
  A pulse in the eternal mind, no less
    Gives somewhere back the thoughts by England given;
Her sights and sounds; dreams happy as her day;
  And laughter, learnt of friends; and gentleness,
    In hearts at peace, under an English heaven.

Rupert Brooke
1887 - 1915

SONNET 5

If I should learn, in some quite casual way,
That you were gone, not to return again -
Read from the back-page of a paper, say,
Held by a neighbour in a subway train,
How at the corner of this avenue
And such a street (so are the papers filled)
A hurrying man, who happened to be you,
At noon today had happened to be killed –
I should not cry aloud—I could not cry
Aloud, or wring my hands in such a place—
I should but watch the station lights rush by
With a more careful interest on my face;
Or raise my eyes and read with greater care
Where to store furs and how to treat the hair.

Edna St Vincent Millay
1892 - 1950

MACBETH, Excerpt One
Act I, Scene VII

Macbeth:

If it were done when 'tis done, then 'twere well
It were done quickly: if the assassination
Could trammel up the consequence, and catch
With his surcease success; that but this blow
Might be the be-all and the end-all here,
But here, upon this bank and shoal of time,
We'd jump the life to come. But in these cases
We still have judgment here; that we but teach
Bloody instructions, which, being taught, return
To plague the inventor: this even-handed justice
Commends th' ingredients of our poison'd chalice
To our own lips. He's here in double trust;
First, as I am his kinsman and his subject,
Strong both against the deed; then, as his host,
Who should against his murderer shut the door,
Not bear the knife myself. Besides, this Duncan
Hath borne his faculties so meek, hath been
So clear in his great office, that his virtues
Will plead like angels, trumpet-tongued, against
The deep damnation of his taking-off;
And pity, like a naked new-born babe,
Striding the blast, or heaven's cherubin, horsed
Upon the sightless couriers of the air,
Shall blow the horrid deed in every eye,
That tears shall drown the wind. I have no spur
To prick the sides of my intent, but only
Vaulting ambition, which o'erleaps itself
And falls on the other -.

William Shakespeare
1564 - 1616

IF NO ONE EVER MARRIES ME

If no one ever marries me –
And I don't see why they should,
For nurse says that I'm not pretty,
And I'm seldom very good –

If no one ever marries me
I shan't mind very much,
I shall buy a squirrel in a cage
And a little rabbit-hutch.

I shall have a cottage near a wood,
And a pony all my own,
And a little lamb, quite clean and tame,
That I can take to town.

And when I'm getting really old –
At twenty-eight or nine –
I shall buy a little orphan-girl
And bring her up as mine.

Lawrence Alma-Tadema
1836 - 1912

IF

If you can keep your head when all about you
Are losing theirs and blaming it on you;
If you can trust yourself when all men doubt you,
But make allowance for their doubting too;
If you can wait and not be tired by waiting,
Or, being lied about, don't deal in lies,
Or, being hated, don't give way to hating,
And yet don't look too good, nor talk too wise;

If you can dream – and not make dreams your master;
If you can think – and not make thoughts your aim;
If you can meet with triumph and disaster
And treat those two impostors just the same;
If you can bear to hear the truth you've spoken
Twisted by knaves to make a trap for fools,
Or watch the things you gave your life to broken,
And stoop and build 'em up with worn out tools;

If you can make one heap of all your winnings
And risk it on one turn of pitch-and-toss,
And lose, and start again at your beginnings
And never breathe a word about your loss;
If you can force your heart and nerve and sinew
To serve your turn long after they are gone,
And so hold on when there is nothing in you
Except the Will which says to them: "Hold on!"

If you can talk with crowds and keep your virtue,
Or walk with kings – nor lose the common touch;
If neither foes nor loving friends can hurt you;
If all men count with you, but none too much;
If you can fill the unforgiving minute
With sixty seconds' worth of distance run –
Yours is the Earth and everything that's in it,
And – which is more – you'll be a Man, my son!

Rudyard Kipling
1865 - 1936

THE BALLAD OF READING GAOL, Excerpt

In Reading gaol by Reading town
  There is a pit of shame,
And in it lies a wretched man
  Eaten by teeth of flame,
In a burning winding-sheet he lies,
  And his grave has got no name.

And there, till Christ call forth the dead,
  In silence let him lie:
No need to waste the foolish tear,
  Or heave the windy sigh:
The man had killed the thing he loved,
  And so he had to die.

And all men kill the thing they love,
  By all let this be heard,
Some do it with a bitter look,
  Some with a flattering word,
The coward does it with a kiss,
  The brave man with a sword!

Oscar Wilde
1854 - 1900

A SHROPSHIRE LAD, Excerpt Two

In summertime on Bredon
    The bells they sound so clear;
Round both the shires they ring them
    In steeples far and near,
    A happy noise to hear.

Here of a Sunday morning
    My love and I would lie,
And see the coloured counties,
    And hear the larks so high
    About us in the sky.

DANE-GELD

It is always a temptation to an armed and agile nation,
    To call upon a neighbour and to say:—
"We invaded you last night—we are quite prepared to fight,
    Unless you pay us cash to go away."

And that is called asking for Dane-geld,
    And the people who ask it explain
That you've only to pay 'em the Dane-geld
    And then you'll get rid of the Dane!

It is always a temptation to a rich and lazy nation,
    To puff and look important and to say:—
"Though we know we should defeat you, we have not the time
                                 to meet you.
    We will therefore pay you cash to go away."

And that is called paying the Dane-geld;
    But we've proved it again and again,
That if once you have paid him the Dane-geld
    You never get rid of the Dane.

It is wrong to put temptation in the path of any nation,
    For fear they should succumb and go astray,
So when you are requested to pay up or be molested,
    You will find it better policy to say:—

"We never pay *any*-one Dane-geld,
    No matter how trifling the cost;
For the end of that game is oppression and shame,
    And the nation that plays it is lost!"

Rudyard Kipling
1865 - 1936

KING JOHN'S CHRISTMAS

King John was not a good man -
He had his little ways.
And sometimes no one spoke to him

For days and days and days.
And men who came across him,
When walking in the town,
Gave him a supercilious stare,
Or passed with noses in the air -
And bad King John stood dumbly there,
Blushing beneath his crown.

King John was not a good man,
And no good friends had he.
He stayed in every afternoon ...
But no one came to tea.
And, round about December,
The cards upon his shelf
Which wished him lots of Christmas cheer,
And fortune in the coming year,
Were never from his near and dear,
But only from himself.

King John was not a good man,
Yet had his hopes and fears.
They'd given him no present now
For years and years and years.
But every year at Christmas,
While minstrels stood about,
Collecting tribute from the young
For all the songs they might have sung,
He stole away upstairs and hung
A hopeful stocking out.

King John was not a good man,
He lived his life aloof;
Alone he thought a message out
While climbing up the roof.
He wrote it down and propped it
Against the chimney stack:
"TO ALL AND SUNDRY – NEAR AND FAR -
F. CHRISTMAS IN PARTICULAR."
And signed it not "Johannes R."
But very humbly, "JACK."

" I want some crackers,
And I want some candy;
I think a box of chocolates
Would come in handy;
I don't mind oranges,
I do like nuts!
And I SHOULD like a pocket-knife
That really cuts.
And, oh! Father Christmas, if you love me at all,
Bring me a big, red india-rubber ball!"

King John was not a good man -
He wrote this message out,
And gat him to his room again,
Descending by the spout.
And all that night he lay there,
A prey to hopes and fears.
"I think that's him a-coming now,

(Anxiety bedewed his brow).
"He'll bring one present, anyhow -
The first I've had for years.

"Forget about the crackers,
And forget about the candy;
I'm sure a box of chocolates
Would never come in handy;
I don't like oranges,
I don't want nuts,
And I HAVE got a pocket-knife
That almost cuts.
But, oh! Father Christmas, if you love me
at all,
Bring me a big, red india-rubber ball!"

King John was not a good man -
Next morning when the sun
Rose up to tell a waiting world
That Christmas had begun,
And people seized their stockings,
And opened them with glee,
And crackers, toys and games appeared,

And lips with sticky sweets were smeared,
King John said grimly: "As I feared,
Nothing again for me!"

"I did want crackers,
And I did want candy;
I know a box of chocolates
Would come in handy;
I do love oranges,
I did want nuts.
I haven't got a pocket-knife -
Not one that cuts.
And, oh! If Father Christmas had loved me at all,
He would have brought a big, red india-rubber ball!"

King John stood by the window,
And frowned to see below
The happy bands of boys and girls
All playing in the snow.
A while he stood there watching,
And envying them all...
When through the window big and red
There hurtled by his royal head,
And bounced and fell upon the bed,
An india-rubber ball!

AND OH, FATHER CHRISTMAS,
MY BLESSINGS ON YOU FALL
FOR BRINGING HIM
A BIG, RED
INDIA-RUBBER
BALL!

A.A. Milne
1882 - 1956

TWO PEARLS

Knowing, fair Sir, my matrimonial thrall,
Two pearls thou sentest me, costly withal,
And I, seeing that love my heart possessed,
I wrapped them coldly in my silken vest.

For mine is a household of high degree,
My husband captain in the King's army;
And me with wit like this should say,
"The troth of wives is forever and ay."

With thy two pearls, I send thee back two tears:
Tears – that we did not meet in earlier years.

Chang Chi
(During Tang Dynasty 618 - 907AD)

THE ROMAN CENTURION'S SONG

(Roman Occupation of Britain AD 300)

Legate, I had the news last night – my cohort ordered home
By ship to Portus Itius and thence by road to Rome.
I've marched the companies aboard, the arms are stowed
                below:
Now let another take my sword. Command me not to go!

I've served in Britain forty years, from Vectis to the Wall,
I have none other home than this, nor any life at all.
Last night I did not understand, but, now the hour draws near
That calls me to my native land, I feel that land is here.

Here where men say my name was made, here where my
                work was done;
Here where my dearest dead are laid – my wife – my wife and
                son;
Here where time, custom, grief and toil, age, memory, service,
                love,
Have rooted me in British soil. Ah, how can I remove?

For me this land, that sea, these airs, those folk and fields
                suffice.
What purple Southern pomp can match our changeful
                Northern skies,
Black with December snows unshed or pearled with August
                haze –
The clanging arch of steel-grey March, or June's long-lighted
                days?

You'll follow widening Rhodanus till vine and olive lean
Aslant before the sunny breeze that sweeps Nemausus clean
To Arelate's triple gate; but let me linger on,
Here where our stiff-necked British oaks confront Euroclydon!

You'll take the old Aurelian Road through shore-descending
                                                pines
Where, blue as any peacock's neck, the Tyrrhene Ocean
                                                shines.
You'll go where laurel crowns are won, but – will you e'er
                                                forget
The scent of hawthorn in the sun, or bracken in the wet?

Let me work here for Britain's sake – at any task you will –
A marsh to drain, a road to make or native troops to drill.
Some Western camp (I know the Pict) or granite Border keep,
Mid seas of heather derelict, where our old messmates sleep.

Legate, I come to you in tears – my cohort ordered home!
I've served in Britain forty years. What should I do in Rome?
Here is my heart, my soul, my mind – the only life I know.
I cannot leave it all behind. Command me not to go!

Rudyard Kipling
1865 - 1936

BAREFOOTED

Let my cottage be one with your mansion,
    You'll own it, so here is my key.
It's yours, and you'll surely maintain it,
    You are richer, and wiser than me.
Then sometimes, at sunrise or sunset,
    You'll walk by barefooted, quite near –
A thing that would never have happened
    If my little boundaries were there.

If your friends come and walk on my flower beds;
    If your children take apples and plums;
Let me say "After all, it's His garden,
    I feed Him if I'm feeding His sons."
Then always, at noon, or at midnight,
    If you pass there, barefooted, I'll know,
And your smile will yield more than my labours,
    And the seedlings I wanted to grow.

If I take down my old barbed-wire fences;
    If I label all "Yours" and not "mine";
If I transfer to you my small treasures,
    And my problems, my worries, my time –
Then some day, by sunlight or starlight
    If you happen to beckon me, I
Will follow, barefooted behind you,
    And learn all you teach me, or try.....
In the All that is part of your Mansion,
    Your garden, Your ocean, Your sky.

Paxye Lucas
1918 - 2003

ELEGY

Let them bury your big eyes
In the secret earth securely,
Your thin fingers, and your fair,
Soft, indefinite-coloured hair -
All of these in some way, surely,
From the secret earth shall rise;
Not for these I sit and stare,
Broken and bereft completely;
Your young flesh that sat so neatly
On your little bones will sweetly
Blossom in the air.

But your voice... never the rushing
Of a river underground,
Not the rising of the wind
In the trees before the rain,
Not the woodcock's watery call,
Not the note the white-throat utters,
Not the feet of children pushing
Yellow leaves along the gutters
In the blue and bitter fall,
Shall content my musing mind
For the beauty of that sound
That in no new way at all
Ever will be heard again.

Sweetly through the sappy stalk
Of the vigorous weed,
Holding all it held before,
Cherished by the faithful sun,
On and on eternally
Shall your altered fluid run,
Bud and bloom and go to seed:
But your singing days are done;
But the music of your talk
Never shall the chemistry
Of the secret earth restore.
All your lovely words are spoken.
Once the ivory box is broken,
Beats the golden bird no more.

Edna St Vincent Millay
1892 - 1950

Lone and alone she lies
    Poor Miss 7,
Five steep flights from the earth,
    And one from heaven;
Dark hair and dark brown eyes, -
Not to be sad she tries,
Still - still it's lonely lies
    Poor Miss 7.

One day-long watch hath she,
        Poor Miss 7,
Not in some orchard sweet
        In April Devon, -
Just four blank walls to see,
And dark come shadowily,
No moon, no stars, ah me!
        Poor Miss 7.

And then to wake again,
        Poor Miss 7,
To the cold night, to have
        Sour physic given;
Out of some dream of pain,
Then strive long hours in vain
Deep dreamless sleep to gain:
        Poor Miss 7.

Yet memory softly sings
        Poor Miss 7,
Songs full of love and peace
        And gladness even;
Clear flowers and tiny wings,
All tender, lovely things,
Hope to her bosom brings---
        Happy Miss 7.

Walter de la Mare
1873 - 1956

A SHROPSHIRE LAD, Excerpt One

Loveliest of trees, the cherry now
Is hung with bloom along the bough,
And stands about the woodland ride
Wearing white for Eastertide.

Now, of my threescore years and ten,
Twenty will not come again,
And take from seventy springs a score,
It only leaves me fifty more.

And since to look at things in bloom
Fifty springs are little room,
About the woodlands I will go
To see the cherry hung with snow.

A.E Housman
1859 - 1936

A SUBALTERN'S LOVE-SONG

Miss J. Hunter Dunn, Miss J. Hunter Dunn,
Furnish'd and burnish'd by Aldershot sun,
What strenuous singles we played after tea,
We in the tournament – you against me!

Love-thirty, love-forty, oh! Weakness of joy,
The speed of a swallow, the grace of a boy,
With carefullest carelessness, gaily you won,
I am weak from your loveliness, Joan Hunter Dunn.

Miss Joan Hunter Dunn, Miss Joan Hunter Dunn
How mad I am, sad I am, glad that you won.
The warm-handled racket is back in its press,
But my shock-headed victor, she loves me no less.

Her father's euonymus shines as we walk,
And swing past the summer-house, buried in talk,
And cool the verandah that welcomes us in
To the six o'clock news and a limejuice and gin.

The scent of the conifers, sound of the bath,
The view from my bedroom of moss-dappled path,
As I struggle with double-end evening tie,
For we dance at the Golf Club, my victor and I.

On the floor of her bedroom lie blazer and shorts
And the cream-coloured walls are be-trophied with sports,
And westering, questioning, settles the sun
On your low-leaded window, Miss Joan Hunter Dunn.

The Hillman is waiting, the light's in the hall,
The pictures of Egypt are bright on the wall.
My sweet, I am standing beside the oak stair
And there on the landing's the light on your hair.

By roads 'not adopted', by woodlanded ways,
She drove to the club in the late summer haze,
Into nine-o'clock Camberley, heavy with bells
And mushroomy, pine-woody, evergreen smells.

Miss Joan Hunter Dunn, Miss Joan Hunter Dunn,
I can hear from the car-park the dance has begun.
Oh! Full Surrey twilight! Importunate band!
Oh! Strongly adorable tennis-girl's hand!

Around us are Rovers and Austins afar,
Above us, the intimate roof of the car,
And here on my right is the girl of my choice,
With the tilt of her nose and the chime of her voice,

And the scent of her wrap, and the words never said,
And the ominous, ominous dancing ahead.
We sat in the car park till twenty to one
And now I'm engaged to Miss Joan Hunter Dunn.

Sir John Betjeman
1906 - 1984

TWELFTH NIGHT, Excerpt
Act I, Scene V

Olivia:
Why, what would you?

Viola:
Make me a willow cabin at your gate,
And call upon my soul within the house;
Write loyal cantons of contemned love,
And sing them loud even in the dead of night;
Halloo your name to the reverberate hills,
And make the babbling gossip of the air
Cry out, 'Olivia!' O, you should not rest
Between the elements of air and earth.
But you should pity me!

William Shakespeare
1564 - 1616

ON FIRST LOOKING INTO CHAPMAN'S HOMER

Much have I travelled in the realms of gold,
  And many goodly states and kingdoms seen;
  Round many western islands have I been
Which bards in fealty to Apollo hold.
Oft of one wide expanse had I been told
  That deep-browed Homer ruled as his demesne;
  Yet did I never breathe its pure serene
Till I heard Chapman speak out loud and bold:
Then felt I like some watcher of the skies
  When a new planet swims into his ken;
Or like stout Cortez when with eagle eyes
  He stared at the Pacific—and all his men
Looked at each other with a wild surmise—
  Silent, upon a peak in Darien.

John Keats
1795 - 1821

FIRST FIG

My candle burns at both ends;
  It will not last the night;
But ah, my foes, and oh, my friends -
  It gives a lovely light!

Edna St Vincent Millay
1892 - 1950

ODE TO A NIGHTINGALE

My heart aches, and a drowsy numbness pains
  My sense, as though of hemlock I had drunk,
Or emptied some dull opiate to the drains
  One minute past, and Lethe-wards had sunk:
'Tis not through envy of thy happy lot,
  But being too happy in thy happiness, --
    That thou, light-winged Dryad of the trees,
        In some melodious plot
Of beechen green, and shadows numberless,
  Singest of summer in full-throated ease.

O for a draught of vintage, that hath been
  Cooled a long age in the deep-delved earth,
Tasting of Flora and the country green,
  Dance, and Provencal song, and sun-burnt mirth!
O for a beaker full of the warm South,
  Full of the true, the blushful Hippocrene,
    With beaded bubbles winking at the brim,
        And purple-stained mouth;
That I might drink, and leave the world unseen,
  And with thee fade away into the forest dim:

Fade far away, dissolve, and quite forget
  What thou among the leaves hast never known,
The weariness, the fever, and the fret
  Here, where men sit and hear each other groan;
Where palsy shakes a few, sad, last grey hairs,
  Where youth grows pale, and spectre-thin, and dies;
    Where but to think is to be full of sorrow
        And leaden-eyed despairs;
Where beauty cannot keep her lustrous eyes,
  Or new love pine at them beyond to-morrow.

Away! Away! For I will fly to thee,
  Not charioted by Bacchus and his pards,
But on the viewless wings of Poesy,
  Though the dull brain perplexes and retards:

Already with thee! Tender is the night,
  And haply the Queen-Moon is on her throne,
    Clustered around by all her starry fays;
        But here there is no light,
Save what from heaven is with the breezes blown
  Through verdurous glooms and winding mossy ways.

I cannot see what flowers are at my feet,
  Nor what soft incense hangs upon the boughs,
But, in embalmed darkness, guess each sweet
  Wherewith the seasonable month endows
The grass, the thicket, and the fruit-tree wild;
  White hawthorne, and the pastoral eglantine;
    Fast-fading violets covered up in leaves;
        And mid-May's eldest child,
The coming musk-rose, full of dewy wine,
  The murmurous haunt of flies on summer eves.

Darkling I listen; and for many a time
  I have been half in love with easeful Death,
Called him soft names in many a mused rhyme,
  To take into the air my quiet breath;
Now more than ever seems it rich to die,
  To cease upon the midnight with no pain,
    While thou art pouring forth thy soul abroad
        In such an ecstasy!
Still wouldst thou sing, and I have ears in vain—
  To thy high requiem become a sod.

Thou wast not born for death, immortal Bird!
  No hungry generations tread thee down;
The voice I hear this passing night was heard
  In ancient days by emperor and clown:
Perhaps the self-same song that found a path
  Through the sad heart of Ruth, when, sick for home,
    She stood in tears amid the alien corn;
        The same that oft-times hath
Charmed magic casements, opening on the foam
  Of perilous seas, in faery lands forlorn.

Forlorn! The very word is like a bell
  To toll me back from thee to my sole self.
Adieu! The fancy cannot cheat so well
  As she is famed to do, deceiving elf.
Adieu! Adieu! Thy plaintive anthem fades
    Past the near meadows, over the still stream,
      Up the hill-side; and now 'tis buried deep
          In the next valley-glades:
Was it a vision, or a waking dream?
    Fled is that music:--do I wake or sleep?

John Keats
1792 - 1821

A BIRTHDAY

My heart is like a singing bird
  Whose nest is in a watered shoot;
My heart is like an apple-tree
  Whose boughs are bent with thick-set fruit;

My heart is like a rainbow shell
  That paddles in a halcyon sea;
My heart is gladder than all these
  Because my love is come to me.

Raise me a dais of silk and down;
  Hang it with vair and purple dyes;
Carve it in doves and pomegranates,
  And peacocks with a hundred eyes;

Work it in gold and silver grapes,
  In leaves and silver fleur-de-lys;
Because the birthday of my life
  Is come, my love is come to me.

Christina Georgina Rossetti
1830 - 1894

82

THE TOYS

My little Son, who look'd from thoughtful eyes
And moved and spoke in quiet grown-up wise,
Having my law the seventh time disobey'd,
I struck him, and dismiss'd
With hard words and unkiss'd,
--His Mother, who was patient, being dead.
Then, fearing lest his grief should hinder sleep,
I visited his bed,
But found him slumbering deep,
With darken'd eyelids, and their lashes yet
From his late sobbing wet.
And I, with moan,
Kissing away his tears, left others of my own;
For, on a table drawn beside his head,
He had put, within his reach,
A box of counters and a red-vein'd stone,
A piece of glass abraded by the beach,
And six or seven shells,
A bottle with bluebells,
And two French copper coins, ranged there with careful art,
To comfort his sad heart.
So when that night I pray'd
To God, I wept, and said:
Ah, when at last we lie with tranced breath,
Not vexing Thee in death,
And Thou rememberest of what toys
We made our joys,
How weakly understood
Thy great commanded good,
Then, fatherly not less
Than I whom Thou hast moulded from the clay,
Thou'lt leave Thy wrath, and say,
'I will be sorry for their childishness.'

Coventry Patmore
1823 - 1896

THE COUNTESS OF PEMBROKE'S ARCADIA,
Excerpt 'The Bargain'

My true love hath my heart, and I have his,
By just exchange one for another given:
I hold his dear, and mine he cannot miss:
There never was a better bargain driven:
My true love hath my heart and I have his.
His heart in me keeps him and me in one,
My heart in him his thoughts and senses guides:
He loves my heart, for once it was his own,
I cherish his because in me it bides:
My true love hath my heart and I have his.

Sir Philip Sidney
1554 - 1586

YIDDLES

Nijinsky danced an awful lot
    And then went off his head
Bronte wrote with passion
    Blue bedsocked in her bed
James Joyce gave us Ulysses
    To show that life's chaotic
Wilde was so unmasculine
    Neiztche was neurotic
An effusive poet bard
    Drank himself erotic
Inchen was incapable
    Without a large narcotic
Tonne died surprisingly
    From pink anti-biotic
Archimedes talked a lot
    Some said he was psychotic

This only goes to prove that
    In a shocking huff
Van Gogh cut his ear off
    Because he'd heard enough.

Patricia M Stott
1935 -

NO, I'M NOT AFRAID

No, I'm not afraid: after a year
Of breathing these prison nights
I will survive into the sadness
To name which is escape.

The cockerel will weep freedom for me
And here – knee-deep in mire –
My gardens shed their water
And the northern air blows in draughts.

And how am I to carry to an alien planet
What are almost tears, as though towards home…
It isn't true, I *am* afraid, my darling!
But make it look as though you haven't noticed.

Irina Ratushinskaya
1954 -

NO WORST

No worst, there is none.
Pitched past pitch of grief,
More pangs will, schooled at forepangs, wilder wring.
Comforter, where, where is your comforting?
Mary, mother of us, where is your relief?
My cries heave, herds-long; huddle in a main, a chief -
Woe, world-sorrow; on an age-old anvil wince and sing –
Then lull, then leave off. Fury had shrieked 'No lingering!

85

Let me be fell: force I must be brief'.
O the mind, mind has mountains; cliffs of fall
Frightful, sheer, no-man-fathomed. Hold them cheap
May who ne'er hung there. Nor does long our small
Durance deal with that steep or deep. Here! Creep,
Wretch, under a comfort serves in a whirlwind: all
Life death does end and each day dies with sleep.

Gerard Manley Hopkins
1844 - 1889

NOT WAVING BUT DROWNING

Nobody heard him, the dead man,
But still he lay moaning:
I was much further out than you thought
And not waving but drowning.

Poor chap, he always loved larking
And now he's dead
It must have been too cold for him his heart gave way,
They said.

Oh, no no no, it was too cold always
(Still the dead one lay moaning)
I was much too far out all my life
And not waving but drowning.

Stevie Smith
1902 - 1971

CARRION COMFORT

Not, I'll not, carrion comfort, Despair, not feast on thee;
Not untwist slack they may be – these last strands of man
In me or, most weary, cry *I can no more.* I can;
Can something, hope, wish day come, not choose not to be.

But ah, but O thou terrible, why wouldst thou rude on me
Thy wring-world right foot rock? lay a lion limb
  against me? scan
With darksome devouring eyes my bruised bones? and fan,
O in turns of tempest, me heaped there; me frantic to
  avoid thee and flee?

Why? That my chaff might fly; my grain lie, sheer and clear.
Nay in all that toil, that coil, since (seems) I kissed the rod,
Hand rather, my heart lo! lapped strength, stole joy,
  would laugh, cheer.
Cheer whom though? the hero whose heaven –
  handling flung me, foot trod
Me? Or me that fought him? O which one? is it each one?
  That night, that year
Of now done darkness I wretch lay wrestling with (my
  God!) my God.

Gerard Manley Hopkins
1844 - 1889

THE JUNGLE BOOK, Excerpt
Mowgli's Brothers (chapter heading)

Now Chil the Kite brings home the night
  That Man the Bat sets free—
The herds are shut in byre and hut,
  For loosed till dawn are we.
This is the hour of pride and power,
  Talon and tush and claw.
Oh, hear the call!—Good hunting all
  That keep the Jungle Law!

Rudyard Kipling
1865 - 1936

CONVERSATION WITH DOG IN PARKED CAR

Now Grandpa's really gone too far!
Into the fleshpots of Leamington Spa!
He only went to buy a bun
(I told him make it only one),
That was an hour and a half ago,
Time for a walk in the park, heyho.

Perhaps some Circe, breathing spice and crooning a ditty,
Has captured my Ulysses, lost in the city?
Perhaps some Siren, tugging at his shirt sleeve
(Did I sew that button on?), promising him summer leave?
Now I see him, careless fellow, sitting in some coral grotto,
Nymphs on knees and draped in grapes, shamelessly
becoming blotto...

Oh, here comes Grandpa—with a crestfallen look,
A bag of nails and a secondhand book.
He shan't go out unaccompanied again
(Freedom frolicking in his brain).
Heaven knows what he'd get up to next!
Lend Grandma your collar and lead, little pet....

Sarah Nock
1935 -

OLD AGE

Now while time darkens
From this twilight
I remember the humming bird
In the noonday
Always in sunlight
Plundering each and every flower.
Even the shadows then
Of those exotic blooms
Were rich and glowing tapestries
When time was young.

Now as the silence deepens
Still I hear the sea that whispers from that soundling shore
With all its promises.
How could I know
Those whispers were but echoes
From an empty shell.

Now that touch is numb
Trailing with trembling fingers on the dry and wrinkled skin
I remember the curved and secret places
Warm and smooth in dawns ago,
And cool the moving air's caress
No claw of Winter gripped me then.

HIGH FLIGHT

O, I have slipped the surly bonds of earth
And danced the skies on laughter silvered wings;
Sunward I've climbed, and joined the tumbling mirth
Of sun-split clouds and done a hundred things
You have not dreamed of – wheeled and soared and swung
High in the sunlit silence
Hovering there, I've chased the shouting wind along, and flung
My eager craft through footless halls of air.
Up, up the long delirious burning blue
I've topped the windswept heights with easy grace
Where never lark, or even eagle flew.
And, while with silent, lifting mind I've trod
The high untrespassed sanctity of space
Put out my hand, and touched the face of God.

John Gillespie Magee Jnr
1922 - 1941

THE SICK ROSE

O Rose, thou art sick!
The invisible worm
That flies in the night,
In the howling storm,

Has found out thy bed
Of crimson joy:
And his dark secret love
Does thy life destroy.

William Blake
1757 - 1827

LORD RANDAL

"O where have you been, Lord Randal, my son?
O where have you been, my handsome young man?"—
"I have been to the wild wood; mother, make my bed soon,
For I'm weary with hunting, and fain would lie down."

"Who gave you your dinner, Lord Randal, my son?
Who gave you your dinner, my handsome young man?"—
"I dined with my sweetheart; mother, make my bed soon,
For I'm weary with hunting, and fain would lie down."

"What had you for dinner, Lord Randal, my son?
What had you for dinner, my handsome young man?"—
"I had eels boiled in broth; mother, make my bed soon,
For I'm weary with hunting, and fain would lie down."

"And where are your bloodhounds, Lord Randal, my son?
And where are your bloodhounds, my handsome young man?"
"O they swelled and they died; mother, make my bed soon,
For I'm weary with hunting, and fain would lie down."

"O I fear you are poisoned, Lord Randal, my son!
O I fear you are poisoned, my handsome young man!"—
"O yes! I am poisoned; mother, make my bed soon,
For I'm sick at the heart, and I fain would lie down."

Anon

TO A FAT LADY SEEN FROM THE TRAIN
Triolet

O why do you walk through the fields in gloves,
    Missing so much and so much?
O fat white woman whom nobody loves,
Why do you walk through the fields in gloves,
When the grass is soft as the breast of doves
    And shivering-sweet to the touch?
O why do you walk through the fields in gloves,
    Missing so much and so much?

Frances Cornford
1886 - 1960

THE KINGDOM OF GOD, Excerpt

O world invisible, we view thee,
    O world intangible, we touch thee,
O world unknowable, we know thee,
    Inapprehensible, we clutch thee!

Does the fish soar to find the ocean,
    The eagle plunge to find the air –
That we ask of the stars in motion
    If they have rumour of thee there?

Not where the wheeling systems darken,
    And our numbed conceiving soars! –
The drift of pinions, would we hearken,
    Beats at our own clay-shuttered doors.

The angels keep their ancient places;-
    Turn but a stone and start a wing!
'Tis ye, 'tis your estrangèd faces,
    That miss the many-splendoured thing.

But (when so sad thou canst not sadder),
    Cry;- and upon thy so sore loss
Shall shine the traffic of Jacob's ladder
    Pitched betwixt Heaven and Charing Cross.

Yea, in the night, my Soul, my daughter,
    Cry—clinging Heaven by the hems;
And lo, Christ walking on the water
    Not of Gennesareth, but Thames!

Francis Thompson
1859 - 1907

COURTESY

Of Courtesy, it is much less
Than Courage of Heart or Holiness,
Yet in my Walks it seems to me
That the Grace of God is in Courtesy.

On Monks I did in Storrington fall,
They took me straight into their Hall;
I saw Three Pictures on a wall,
And Courtesy was in them all.

The first the Annunciation;
The second the Visitation;
The third the Consolation,
Of God that was our Lady's Son.

The first was of Saint Gabriel;
On Wings a-flame from Heaven he fell
And as he went upon one knee
He shone with Heavenly Courtesy.

95

Our Lady out of Nazareth rode –
It was her month of heavy load;
Yet was her Face both great and kind,
For Courtesy was in Her Mind.

The third it was our Little Lord,
Whom all the Kings in arms adored;
He was so small you could not see
His large intent of Courtesy.

Our Lord, that was our Lady's Son,
Go bless you, People, one by one;
My Rhyme is written, my work is done.

Hilaire Belloc
1870 - 1953

OH, FOR THE TIME WHEN I SHALL SLEEP

Oh, for the time when I shall sleep
    Without identity,
And never care how rain may steep,
    Or snow may cover me!
No promised heaven, these wild desires
    Could all, or half fulfil;
No threatened hell, with quenchless fires,
    Subdue this quenchless will!

So said I, and still say the same;
    Still, to my death, will say—
Three gods, within this little frame,
    Are warring night and day;
Heaven could not hold them all, and yet
    They all are held in me;
And must be mine till I forget
    My present entity!

Oh, for the time, when in my breast
    Their struggles will be o'er!
Oh, for the day when I shall rest,
    And never suffer more!

Emily Bronte
1818 - 1848

SONNET 21

Oh, my beloved, have you thought of this:
How in the years to come unscrupulous Time,
More cruel than Death, will tear you from my kiss,
And make you old, and leave me in my prime?
How you and I, who scale together yet
A little while the sweet, immortal height
No pilgrim may remember or forget,
As sure as the world turns, some granite night
Shall lie awake and know the gracious flame
Gone out forever on the mutual stone;
And call to mind how on the day you came
I was a child, and you a hero grown?
And the night pass, and the strange morning break
Upon our anguish for each other's sake!

Edna St Vincent Millay
1892 - 1950

DARK TO DARK

Oh night wind why do you blow so coldly
From the beautiful day that was my life.
Must I wait the dark boatman to take me
Over the river so many have crossed?
Can I not be spared yet one more day
For all the lives I have not led?
Is there no dew at dawn
That I may print my foot once more
Among the gossamer of other lives?
Is there no single skylark left to sing to me?
No dolphin who will leap
To splinter diamonds from the deep?
No hand to hold
No voice to speak
No tear to glisten on the cheek?

So brief the time from dark to dark
And yet that time unique to me
Contained a universe.

I think I hear the oars that splash the night
Has he come
To take me to oblivion?

Peter Perrin
1917 -

HOME THOUGHTS FROM ABROAD

Oh, to be in England
Now that April's there,
And whoever wakes in England
Sees, some morning, unaware,
That the lowest boughs and the brushwood sheaf
Round the elm-tree bole are in tiny leaf,
While the chaffinch sings on the orchard bough
In England—now!

And after April, when May follows,
And the whitethroat builds, and all the swallows!
Hark, where my blossomed pear-tree in the hedge
Leans to the field and scatters on the clover
Blossoms and dewdrops—at the bent spray's edge—
That's the wise thrush; he sings each song twice over,
Lest you should think he never could recapture
That first fine careless rapture!
And though the fields look rough with hoary dew,
All will be gay when noontide wakes anew
The buttercups, the little children's dower
--Far brighter than this gaudy melon-flower!

Robert Browning
1812 - 1889

LA BELLE DAME SANS MERCI

Oh what can ail thee, knight-at-arms,
    Alone and palely loitering?
The sedge is wither'd from the lake,
        And no birds sing.

O what can ail thee, knight-at arms,
    So haggard and so woe-begone?
The squirrel's granary is full,
        And the harvest's done.

I see a lily on thy brow
    With anguish moist and fever dew;
And on thy cheek a fading rose
        Fast withereth too.

"I met a lady in the meads,
    Full beautiful—a faery's child,
Her hair was long, her foot was light,
        And her eyes were wild

"I made a garland for her head,
    And bracelets too, and fragrant zone;
She look'd at me as she did love,
        And made sweet moan.

"I set her on my pacing steed
    And nothing else saw all day long,
For sideways would she lean, and sing
        A faery's song.

"She found me roots of relish sweet,
    And honey wild and manna dew,
And sure in language strange she said,
        'I love thee true!'

"She took me to her elfin grot,
    And there she wept and sigh'd full sore;
And there I shut her wild, wild eyes
        With kisses four.

"And there she lulled me asleep,
    And there I dream'd—Ah! woe betide!
The latest dream I ever dream'd
        On the cold hill's side.

"I saw pale kings and princes too,
    Pale warriors, death-pale were they all;
Who cried—'La belle Dame sans Merci
        Hath thee in thrall!'

"I saw their starved lips in the gloam
    With horrid warning gaped wide,
And I awoke and found me here
        On the cold hill's side.

"And this is why I sojourn here
    Alone and palely loitering,
Though the sedge is wither'd from the lake,
        And no birds sing."

John Keats
1795 - 1821

ON THE BEACH AT NIGHT

On the beach, at night,
Stands a child, with her father,
Watching the east, the autumn sky.

Up through the darkness,
While ravening clouds, the burial clouds, in black masses
                                spreading,
Lower, sullen and fast, athwart and down the sky,
Amid a transparent clear belt of ether yet left in the east,
Ascends, large and calm, the lord-star Jupiter;
And nigh at hand, only a very little above,
Swim the delicate sisters, the Pleiades.

SUMMUM BONUM, Excerpt

One who never turned his back but marched breast forward,
    Never doubted clouds would break,
Never dreamed, though right were worsted, wrong would
                                        triumph,
    Held we fall to rise, are baffled to fight better,
        Sleep to wake.

Robert Browning
1812 - 1889

SONNET 15

Only until this cigarette is ended,
A little moment at the end of all,
While on the floor the quiet ashes fall,
And in the firelight to a lance extended,
Bizarrely with the jazzing music blended,
The broken shadow dances on the wall,
I will permit my memory to recall
The vision of you, by all my dreams attended.
And then adieu, - farewell! – the dream is done.
Yours is a face of which I can forget
The colour and the features, every one,
The words not ever, and the smiles not yet;
But in your day this moment is the sun
Upon a hill, after the sun has set.

Edna St Vincent Millay
1892 - 1950

INTIMATIONS OF IMMORTALITY, Excerpt Two

Our birth is but a sleep and a forgetting:
The Soul that rises with us, our life's Star,
Hath had elsewhere its setting,
And cometh from afar:
Not in entire forgetfulness,
And not in utter nakedness,
But trailing clouds of glory do we come
From God, who is our home:
Heaven lies about us in our infancy!
Shades of the prison-house begin to close
Upon the growing Boy,
But He beholds the light, and whence it flows,
He sees it in his joy;
The Youth, who daily farther from the east
Must travel, still is Nature's priest,
And by the vision splendid
Is on his way attended;
At length the Man perceives it die away,
And fade into the light of common day.

William Wordsworth
1770 - 1850

THE GLORY OF THE GARDEN

Our England is a garden that is full of stately views,
Of borders, beds and shrubberies and lawns and avenues,
With statues on the terraces and peacocks strutting by;
But the Glory of the Garden lies in more than meets the eye.

For where the old thick laurels grow, along the thin red wall,
You will find the tool – and potting-sheds which are the heart
of all;
The cold-frames and the hot-houses, the dungpits and the
tanks,
The rollers, carts and drain-pipes, with the barrows and the
planks.

And there you'll see the gardeners, the men and 'prentice
boys
Told off to do as they are bid and do it without noise;
For, except when seeds are planted and we shout to scare the
birds,
The Glory of the Garden it abideth not in words.

And some can pot begonias and some can bud a rose,
And some are hardly fit to trust with anything that grows;
But they can roll and trim the lawns and sift the sand and
loam,
For the Glory of the Garden occupieth all who come.

Our England is a garden, and such gardens are not made
By singing:- "Oh, how beautiful!" and sitting in the shade,
While better men than we go out and start their working lives
At grubbing weeds from gravel-paths with broken dinner
-knives.

There's not a pair of legs so thin, there's not a head so thick,
There's not a hand so weak and white, nor yet a heart so sick,
But it can find some needful job that's crying to be done,
For the Glory of the Garden glorifieth every one.

Then seek your job with thankfulness and work till further
                                    orders,
If it's only netting strawberries or killing slugs on borders;
And when your back stops aching and your hands begin to
                                    harden,
You will find yourself a partner in the Glory of the Garden.

Oh, Adam was a gardener, and God who made him sees
That half a proper gardener's work is done upon his knees,
So when your work is finished, you can wash your hands and
                                    pray
For the Glory of the Garden, that it may not pass away!
And the Glory of the Garden it shall never pass away!

                                        Rudyard Kipling
                                        1865 - 1936

INVICTUS

Out of the night that covers me,
    Black as the pit from pole to pole,
I thank whatever gods may be
    For my unconquerable soul.

In the fell clutch of circumstance
    I have not winced nor cried aloud.
Under the bludgeonings of chance
    My head is bloody, but unbow'd.

Beyond this place of wrath and tears
    Looms but the Horror of the shade,
And yet the menace of the years
    Finds and shall find me unafraid.

It matters not how strait the gate,
    How charged with punishments the scroll,
I am the master of my fate:
    I am the captain of my soul.

William Ernest Henley
1849 - 1903

SONNET 29

Pity me not because the light of day
At close of day no longer walks the sky;
Pity me not for beauties passed away
From field and thicket as the years go by;
Pity me not the waning of the moon,
Nor that the ebbing tide goes out to sea,
Nor that a man's desire is hushed so soon,
And you no longer look with love on me.
This have I known always: Love is no more
Than the wide blossom which the wind assails,
Than the great tide that treads the shifting shore,
Strewing fresh wreckage gathered in the gales:
Pity me that the heart is slow to learn
What the swift mind beholds at every turn.

Edna St Vincent Millay
1892 - 1950

CARGOES

Quinquireme of Nineveh from distant Ophir
Rowing home to haven in sunny Palestine,
      With a cargo of ivory,
      And apes and peacocks,
Sandalwood, cedarwood, and sweet white wine.

Stately Spanish galleon coming from the Isthmus,
Dipping through the Tropics by the palm-green shores,
      With a cargo of diamonds,
      Emeralds, amethysts,
Topazes, and cinnamon, and gold moidores.

Dirty British coaster with a salt-caked smoke stack
Butting through the Channel in the mad March days,
      With a cargo of Tyne coal,
      Road-rail, pig-lead,
Firewood, iron-ware, and cheap tin trays.

John Masefield
1878 - 1967

THE OLD STOIC

    Riches I hold in light esteem,
        And love I laugh to scorn;
    And lust of fame was but a dream,
        That vanished with the morn:

    And if I pray, the only prayer
        That moves my lips for me
    Is, "Leave the heart that now I bear,
        And give me liberty!"

Yes, as my swift days near their goal,
    'Tis all that I implore;
In life and death a chainless soul,
    With courage to endure.

Emily Bronte
1818 - 1848

SAY NOT THE STRUGGLE NAUGHT AVAILETH

Say not the struggle naught availeth,
    The labour and the wounds are vain,
The enemy faints not, nor faileth,
    And as things have been, things remain.

If hopes were dupes, fears may be liars;
    It may be, in yon smoke concealed,
Your comrades chase e'en now the fliers,
    And, but for you, possess the field.

For while the tired waves, vainly breaking,
    Seem here no painful inch to gain,
Far back through creeks and inlets making
    Comes, silent, flooding in, the main,

And not by eastern windows only,
    When daylight comes, comes in the light,
In front the sun climbs slow, how slowly,
    But westward, look, the land is bright.

Arthur Hugh Clough
1819 - 1861

ODE TO AUTUMN

Season of mists and mellow fruitfulness!
    Close bosom-friend of the maturing sun;
Conspiring with him how to load and bless
    With fruit the vines that round the thatch-eaves run;
To bend with apples the moss'd cottage-trees,
    And fill all fruit with ripeness to the core;
        To swell the gourd, and plump the hazel shells
    With a sweet kernel; to set budding more,
And still more, later flowers for the bees,
Until they think warm days will never cease,
        For summer has o'er-brimmed their clammy cells.

Who has not seen thee oft amid thy store?
    Sometimes whoever seeks abroad may find
Thee sitting careless on a granary floor,
    Thy hair soft-lifted by the winnowing wind;
Or on a half-reaped furrow sound asleep,
    Drowsed with the fume of poppies, while thy hook
        Spares the next swath and all its twined flowers;
    And sometime like a gleaner thou dost keep
Steady thy laden head across a brook;
Or by a cider-press, with patient look,
        Thou watchest the last oozings, hours by hours.

Where are the songs of Spring? Ay, where are they?
    Think not of them, thou hast thy music too,
While barred clouds bloom the soft-dying day,
    And touch the stubble-plains with rosy hue;
Then in a wailful choir, the small gnats mourn
    Among the river sallows, borne aloft
        Or sinking as the light wind lives or dies;
    And full-grown lambs loud bleat from hilly bourn;
Hedge-crickets sing; and now with treble soft
The redbreast whistles from a garden-croft,
        And gathering swallows twitter in the skies.

John Keats
1795 - 1821

THE LADY OF SHALOTT, Excerpt

She left the web, she left the loom,
She made three paces thro' the room,
She saw the water-lily bloom,
She saw the helmet and the plume,
    She look'd down to Camelot.
Out flew the web and floated wide;
The mirror crack'd from side to side
'The curse is come upon me!' cried
    The Lady of Shalott.

In the stormy east-wind straining,
The pale yellow woods were waning,
The broad stream in his banks complaining,
Heavily the low sky raining
    Over tower'd Camelot;
Down she came and found a boat
Beneath a willow left afloat,
And round about the prow she wrote
    The Lady of Shalott.

And down the river's dim expanse –
Like some bold seer in a trance,
Seeing all his own mischance—
With a glassy countenance
    Did she look to Camelot.
And at the closing of the day
She loosed the chain, and down she lay;
The broad stream bore her far away,
    The Lady of Shalott.

Lying, robed in snowy white
That loosely flew to left and right—
The leaves upon her falling light—
Thro' the noises of the night
    She floated down to Camelot:
And as the boat-head wound along
The willowy hills and fields among,
They heard her singing her last song,
    The Lady of Shalott.

Heard a carol, mournful, holy,
Chanted loudly, chanted lowly,
Till her blood was frozen slowly,
And her eyes were darken'd wholly,
     Turn'd to tower'd Camelot;
For ere she reach'd upon the tide
The first house by the water-side,
Singing in her song she died,
     The Lady of Shalott.

Under tower and balcony,
By garden-wall and gallery,
A gleaming shape she floated by,
Dead-pale between the houses high,
     Silent into Camelot.
Out upon the wharfs they came,
Knight and burgher, lord and dame,
And round the prow they read her name,
     The Lady of Shalott.

Who is this? And what is here?
And in the lighted palace near
Died the sound of royal cheer;
And they cross'd themselves for fear,
     All the knights at Camelot:
But Lancelot mused a little space;
He said, 'She has a lovely face;
God in His mercy lend her grace,
     The Lady of Shalott.'

Alfred, Lord Tennyson
1809 - 1892

MACBETH, Excerpt Two
Act V, Scene V

Macbeth:

She should have died hereafter;
There would have been a time for such a word.
To-morrow, and to-morrow, and to-morrow,
Creeps in this petty pace from day to day,
To the last syllable of recorded time;
And all our yesterdays have lighted fools
The way to dusty death. Out, out, brief candle!
Life's but a walking shadow, a poor player
That struts and frets his hour upon the stage,
And then is heard no more: it is a tale
Told by an idiot, full of sound and fury,
Signifying nothing.

William Shakespeare
1564 - 1616

MISTLETOE

Sitting under the mistletoe
(Pale-green fairy mistletoe),
One last candle burning low,
All the sleepy dancers gone,
Just one candle burning on,
Shadows lurking everywhere:
Some one came, and kissed me there.

Tired I was; my head would go
Nodding under the mistletoe
(Pale-green, fairy mistletoe);
No footsteps came, no voice, but only
Just as I sat there, sleepy, lonely,
Stooped in the still and shadowy air
Lips unseen—and kissed me there.

Walter de la Mare
1873 - 1956

PIANO

Softly, in the dusk, a woman is singing to me;
Taking me back down the vista of years, till I see
A child sitting under the piano, in the boom of the tingling
                                                    strings
And pressing the small, poised feet of a mother who smiles as
                                                    she sings.

In spite of myself, the insidious mastery of song
Betrays me back, till the heart of me weeps to belong
To the old Sunday evenings at home, with winter outside
And hymns in the cosy parlour, the tinkling piano our guide.

So now it is vain for the singer to burst into clamour
With the great black piano appassionato. The glamour
Of childish days is upon me, my manhood is cast
Down in the flood of remembrance, I weep like a child for the
                                                    past.

                                                    D.H. Lawrence
                                                    1885 - 1930

SONG

Stop all the clocks, cut off the telephone,
Prevent the dog from barking with a juicy bone,
Silence the pianos and with muffled drum
Bring out the coffin, let the mourners come.

Let aeroplanes circle moaning overhead
Scribbling on the sky the message He Is Dead,
Put crepe bows round the white necks of the public doves,
Let the traffic policemen wear black cotton gloves.

116

He was my North, my South, my East and West,
My working week and my Sunday rest,
My noon, my midnight, my talk, my song;
I thought that love would last for ever: I was wrong.

The stars are not wanted now; put out every one,
Pack up the moon and dismantle the sun,
Pour away the ocean and sweep up the wood;
For nothing now can ever come to any good.

W.H. Auden
1907 - 1973

CROSSING THE BAR

Sunset and evening star,
And one clear call for me!
And may there be no moaning of the bar,
When I put out to sea.

But such a tide as moving seems asleep,
Too full for sound and foam,
When that which drew from out the boundless deep
Turns again home.

Twilight and evening bell,
And after that the dark!
And may there be no sadness of farewell,
When I embark;

For tho' from out our bourne of Time and Place
The flood may bear me far,
I hope to see my Pilot face to face
When I have crost the bar.

Alfred, Lord Tennyson
1809 - 1892

THE PRINCESS, Excerpt

Tears, idle tears, I know not what they mean,
Tears from the depth of some divine despair
Rise in the heart, and gather to the eyes,
In looking on the happy autumn-fields,
And thinking of the days that are no more.

Fresh as the first beam glittering on a sail,
That brings our friends up from the underworld,
Sad as the last which reddens over one
That sinks with all we love below the verge;
So sad, so fresh, the days that are no more.

Ah, sad and strange as in dark summer dawns
The earliest pipe of half-awakened birds
To dying ears, when unto dying eyes
The casement slowly grows a glimmering square;
So sad, so strange, the days that are no more.

Dear as remembered kisses after death,
And sweet as those by hopeless fancy feigned
On lips that are for others; deep as love,
Deep as first love, and wild with all regret;
O Death in Life, the days that are no more!

Alfred, Lord Tennyson
1809 - 1892

MY LAST DUCHESS

That's my last Duchess painted on the wall,
Looking as if she were alive. I call
That piece a wonder, now: Fra Pandolf's hands
Worked busily a day, and there she stands.
Will't please you sit and look at her? I said
'Fra Pandolf' by design, for never read
Strangers like you that pictured countenance,
The depth and passion of its earnest glance,
But to myself they turned (since none puts by
The curtain I have drawn for you, but I)
And seemed as they would ask me, if they durst,
How such a glance came there; so, not the first
Are you to turn and ask thus. Sir, 't was not
Her husband's presence only, called that spot
Of joy into the Duchess' cheek: perhaps
Fra Pandolf chanced to say "Her mantle laps
Over my lady's wrist too much," or "Paint
Must never hope to reproduce the faint
Half-flush that dies along her throat:" such stuff
Was courtesy, she thought, and cause enough
For calling up that spot of joy. She had
A heart... how shall I say... ? — too soon made glad,
Too easily impressed; she liked whate'er
She looked on, and her looks went everywhere.
Sir, 'twas all one! My favour at her breast,
The drooping of the daylight in the West,
The bough of cherries some officious fool
Broke in the orchard for her, the white mule
She rode with round the terrace - all and each
Would draw from her alike the approving speech,
Or blush, at least. She thanked men, — good; but thanked...
Somehow... I know not how... as if she ranked
My gift of a nine hundred years old name
With anybody's gift. Who'd stoop to blame
This sort of trifling? Even had you skill
In speech — (which I have not) — to make your will
Quite clear to such a one, and say, "Just this
Or that in you disgusts me; here you miss,

Or there exceed the mark" — and if she let
Herself be lessoned so, nor plainly set
Her wits to yours, forsooth, and made excuse,
— E'en then would be some stooping, and I choose
Never to stoop.   Oh, Sir, she smiled, no doubt,
Whene'er I passed her; but who passed without
Much the same smile?   This grew; I gave commands;
Then all smiles stopped together.   There she stands
As if alive.   Will't please you rise?   We'll meet
The company below, then.   I repeat,
The Count your Master's known munificence
Is ample warrant that no just pretence
Of mine for dowry will be disallowed;
Though his fair daughter's self, as I avowed
At starting, is my object.   Nay, we'll go
Together down, Sir!   Notice Neptune, though,
Taming a sea-horse, thought a rarity,
Which Claus of Innsbruck cast in bronze for me!

Robert Browning
1812 - 1889

THE DESTRUCTION OF SENNACHERIB

The Assyrian came down like the wolf on the fold,
And his cohorts were gleaming in purple and gold;
And the sheen of their spears was like stars on the sea,
When the blue wave rolls nightly on deep Galilee.

Like the leaves of the forest when Summer is green,
That host with their banners at sunset were seen:
Like the leaves of the forest when Autumn hath blown,
That host on the morrow lay withered and strown.

120

For the Angel of Death spread his wings on the blast,
And breathed in the face of the foe as he pass'd;
And the eyes of the sleepers wax'd deadly and chill,
And their hearts but once heaved, and forever grew still!

And there lay the steed with his nostril all wide;
But through it there roll'd not the breath of his pride:
And the foam of his gasping lay white on the turf,
And cold as the spray of the rock-beating surf.

And there lay the rider, distorted and pale,
With the dew on his brow, and the rust on his mail,
And the tents were all silent, the banners alone,
The lances unlifted, the trumpet unblown.

And the widows of Ashur are loud in their wail;
And the idols are broke in the temples of Baal;
And the might of the Gentile, unsmote by the sword,
Hath melted like snow in the glance of the Lord!

George Gordon, Lord Byron
1788 - 1824

CHRISTMAS

The bells of waiting Advent ring,
    The Tortoise stove is lit again
And lamp-oil light across the night
    Has caught the streaks of winter rain
In many a stained-glass window sheen
From Crimson Lake to Hooker's Green.

The holly in the windy hedge
    And round the Manor House the yew
Will soon be stripped to deck the ledge,
    The altar, font and arch and pew,
So that the villagers can say
'The Church looks nice' on Christmas Day.

Provincial public houses blaze
    And Corporation tramcars clang,
On lighted tenements I gaze
    Where paper decorations hang.
And bunting in the red Town Hall
Says 'Merry Christmas to you all'.

And London shops on Christmas Eve
    Are strung with silver bells and flowers
As hurrying clerks the City leave
    To pigeon-haunted classic towers
And marbled clouds go scudding by
The many-steepled London sky.

And girls in slacks remember Dad,
    And oafish louts remember Mum,
And sleepless children's hearts are glad,
    And Christmas-morning bells say 'come!'
Even to shining ones who dwell
Safe in the Dorchester Hotel.

And is it true? And is it True,
    This most tremendous tale of all,
Seen in a stained glass window's hue,
    A Baby in an ox's stall?
The maker of the stars and sea
Become a Child on earth for me?

And is it true? For if it is,
    No loving fingers tying strings
Around those tissued fripperies,
    The sweet and silly Christmas things,
Bath salts and inexpensive scent
And hideous tie so kindly meant.

No love that in a family dwells,
    No carolling in frosty air,
Nor all the steeple shaking bells
    Can with this single Truth compare —
That God was Man in Palestine
And lives today in Bread and Wine.

Sir John Betjeman
1906 - 1984

HOW THE CAMEL GOT HIS HUMP
from the JUST-SO STORIES

The Camel's hump is an ugly lump
Which well you may see at the Zoo;
But uglier yet is the hump we get
From having too little to do.

Kiddies and grown-ups too-oo-oo,
If we haven't enough to do-oo-oo,
We get the hump -
Cameelious hump -
The hump that is black and blue!

We climb out of bed with a frouzly head
And a snarly-yarly voice.
We shiver and scowl and we grunt and we growl
At our bath and our boots and our toys;

And there ought to be a corner for me
(And I know there is one for you)
When we get the hump -
Cameelious hump -
The hump that is black and blue!

The cure for this ill is not to sit still,
Or frowst with a book by the fire;
But to take a large hoe and a shovel also,
And dig till you gently perspire;

And then you will find that the sun and the wind,
And the Djinn of the Garden too,
Have lifted the hump -
The horrible hump -
The hump that is black and blue!

I get it as well as you-oo-oo-
If I haven't enough to do-oo-oo!
We all get hump -
Cameelious hump -
Kiddies and grown-ups too!

Rudyard Kipling
1865 - 1936

BIRDS, BAGS, BEARS AND BUNS

The common cormorant or shag
Lays eggs inside a paper bag.
The reason you will see no doubt,
It is to keep the lightning out,
But what these unobservant birds
Have never noticed is that herds
Of wandering bears may come with buns
And steal the bags to hold the crumbs.

Anon

CODE POEM FOR THE FRENCH RESISTANCE

The life that I have is all that I have
And the life that I have is yours.
The love that I have of the life that I have
Is yours and yours and yours.

A sleep I shall have
A rest I shall have,
Yet death will be but a pause,
For the peace of my years in the long green grass
Will be yours and yours and yours.

Leo Marks
1920 - 2001

SHADOWY KINGS

The morning lies unspoiled
By man's activities
And only birds find chinks
In the silent dawn.
Now they come; wild geese;
Cranking the day
With a ratcheting call
And the air is sawn
Into mystical sudden divide.

They tear into early mist
Till above my head
The crescendo is fanned
By the rhythm of wings
Blurring the mind
Of everything but these
Airborne shadowy kings
Who rule in a passing arrow.

Sweeping an arc
Through sky-wide paths
With nothing to guide
But outstretched necks
They fly in pattern
Till the splintered skein
Becomes distant specks
And the morning calms once more.

Jennie Horsman
1937 -

THE MERCHANT OF VENICE, Excerpt
Act IV, Scene I

Portia:

The quality of mercy is not strain'd,
It droppeth as the gentle rain from heaven
Upon the place beneath: it is twice bless'd;
It blesseth him that gives and him that takes:
'Tis mightiest in the mightiest: it becomes
The throned monarch better than his crown;
His sceptre shows the force of temporal power,
The attribute to awe and majesty,
Wherein doth sit the dread and fear of kings;
But mercy is above this sceptred sway,
It is enthroned in the heart of kings,
It is an attribute to God himself,
And earthly power doth then show likest God's
When mercy seasons justice. Therefore, Jew,
Though justice be thy plea, consider this,
That in the course of justice none of us
Should see salvation: we do pray for mercy,
And that same prayer doth teach us all to render
The deeds of mercy.

William Shakespeare
1564 - 1616

DOVER BEACH

The sea is calm tonight.
The tide is full, the moon lies fair
Upon the Straits—on the French coast the light
Gleams, and is gone; the cliffs of England stand,
Glimmering and vast, out in the tranquil bay.

126

Come to the window, sweet is the night air!
Only, from the long line of spray
Where the sea meets the moon-blanched sand,
Listen! You hear the grating roar
Of pebbles which the waves suck back, and fling,
At their return, up the high strand,
Begin, and cease, and then again begin,
With tremulous cadence slow, and bring
The eternal note of sadness in.

Sophocles long ago
Heard it on the Aegean, and it brought
Into his mind the turbid ebb and flow
Of human misery; we
Find also in the sound a thought,
Hearing it by this distant northern sea.

The Sea of Faith
Was once, too, at the full, and round earth's shore
Lay like the folds of a bright girdle furled;
But now I only hear
Its melancholy, long, withdrawing roar,
Retreating to the breath
Of the night-wind down the vast edges drear
And naked shingles of the world.

Ah, love, let us be true
To one another! for the world, which seems
To lie before us like a land of dreams,
So various, so beautiful, so new,
Hath really neither joy, nor love, nor light,
Nor certitude, nor peace, nor help for pain;
And we are here as on a darkling plain
Swept with confused alarms of struggle and flight,
Where ignorant armies clash by night.

Matthew Arnold
1822 - 1888

BLOW, BUGLE, BLOW
Song from 'The Princess'

The splendour falls on castle walls
    And snowy summits old in story:
The long light shakes across the lakes,
    And the wild cataract leaps in glory.
Blow, bugle, blow, set the wild echoes flying,
Blow, bugle; answer, echoes, dying, dying, dying.

O hark, O hear! how thin and clear,
    And thinner, clearer, farther going!
O sweet and far from cliff and scar
    The horns of Elfland faintly blowing!
Blow, let us hear the purple glens replying:
Blow bugle; answer, echoes, dying, dying, dying.

O love, they die in yon rich sky,
    They faint on hill or field or river:
Our echoes roll from soul to soul,
    And grow for ever and for ever.
Blow, bugle, blow, set the wild echoes flying,
And answer, echoes, answer, dying, dying, dying.

Alfred, Lord Tennyson
1809 - 1892

THE WALRUS AND THE CARPENTER
(from 'Through the Looking-Glass and What Alice Found
There')

The sun was shining on the sea,
Shining with all his might:
He did his very best to make
The billows smooth and bright —
And this was odd, because it was
The middle of the night.

The moon was shining sulkily,
Because she thought the sun
Had got no business to be there
After the day was done —
"It's very rude of him," she said,
"To come and spoil the fun!"

The sea was wet as wet could be,
The sands were dry as dry.
You could not see a cloud, because
No cloud was in the sky:
No birds were flying overhead -
There were no birds to fly.

The Walrus and the Carpenter
Were walking close at hand;
They wept like anything to see
Such quantities of sand:
"If this were only cleared away,"
They said, "it would be grand!"

"If seven maids with seven mops
Swept it for half a year,
Do you suppose," the Walrus said,
"That they could get it clear?"
"I doubt it," said the Carpenter,
And shed a bitter tear.

"O Oysters, come and walk with us!"
The Walrus did beseech.
"A pleasant walk, a pleasant talk,
Along the briny beach:
We cannot do with more than four,
To give a hand to each."

The eldest Oyster looked at him,
But never a word he said:
The eldest Oyster winked his eye,
And shook his heavy head —
Meaning to say he did not choose
To leave the oyster-bed.

But four young Oysters hurried up,
All eager for the treat;
Their coats were brushed, their faces washed,
Their shoes were clean and neat —
And this was odd, because, you know,
They hadn't any feet.

Four other Oysters followed them,
And yet another four;
And thick and fast they came at last,
And more, and more, and more —
All hopping through the frothy waves,
And scrambling to the shore.

The Walrus and the Carpenter
Walked on a mile or so,
And then they rested on a rock
Conveniently low:
And all the little Oysters stood
And waited in a row.

"The time has come," the Walrus said,
"To talk of many things:
Of shoes — and ships — and sealing wax -
Of cabbages — and kings —
And why the sea is boiling hot -
And whether pigs have wings."

"But wait a bit," the Oysters cried,
"Before we have our chat;
For some of us are out of breath,
And all of us are fat!"
"No hurry!" said the Carpenter.
They thanked him much for that.

"A loaf of bread," the Walrus said,
"Is what we chiefly need:
Pepper and vinegar besides
Are very good indeed —
Now if you're ready, Oysters dear,
We can begin to feed."

"But not on us!" the Oysters cried,
Turning a little blue.
"After such kindness, that would be
A dismal thing to do!"
"The night is fine," the Walrus said.
"Do you admire the view?

"It was so kind of you to come,
And you are very nice!"
The Carpenter said nothing but
"Cut us another slice:
I wish you were not quite so deaf —
I've had to ask you twice!"

"It seems a shame," the Walrus said,
"To play them such a trick,
After we've brought them out so far,
And made them trot so quick!"
The Carpenter said nothing but
"The butter's spread too thick!"

"I weep for you," the Walrus said:
"I deeply sympathize."
With sobs and tears he sorted out
Those of the largest size,
Holding his pocket-handkerchief
Before his streaming eyes.

"O Oysters," said the Carpenter,
"You've had a pleasant run!
Shall we be trotting home again?"
But answer came there none —
And this was scarcely odd, because
They'd eaten every one.

Lewis Carroll
1832 - 1898

PRAYER FOR A NEW MOTHER

The things she knew, let her forget again —
The voices in the sky, the fear, the cold,
The gaping shepherds, and the queer old men
Piling their clumsy gifts of foreign gold.

Let her have laughter with her little one:
Teach her the endless, tuneless songs to sing,
Grant her the right to whisper to her son
The foolish names one dare not call a king.

Keep from her dreams the rumble of a crowd,
The smell of rough-cut wood, the trail of red,
The thick and chilly whiteness of the shroud
That wraps the strange new body of the dead.

Ah, let her go, kind Lord, where mothers go
And boast his pretty words and ways, and plan
The proud and happy years that they shall know
Together, when her son is grown a man.

Dorothy Parker
1893 - 1967

A SOLUTION

The world contains so many beautiful things to gaze at
That gazing is an occupation that you could spend days at,
And these beautiful things are of so many different kinds, or
        shall we say heterogeneous,
Such as the sun and moon etc. and butterflies and mermaids
        etc. that to list them all you would have to be an
        etcetera genius
So I shall hasten to a landing
And mention two beautiful things that are to my mind
        outstanding,
And one of them is to be on a train,
And see what we see when we flatten our noses against the
        pane,
And the other is wistful enough to make anybody feel cosmic
        and pious.
Which is to stand beside the track and wave at the passengers
        as they rocket by us,
So that is why rather than be an etcetera or any other kind of
        genius
I would rather be schizophrenious,
Because I should regard it as the most satisfactory of stunts
To be able to split my personality and be in two places at
        once,
For who could be so happy as I
Sitting with nose against a train window watching me wave to
        me as I go rocketing by?

Attr. *Ogden Nash*
1902 - 1971

GOD'S GRANDEUR

The world is charged with the grandeur of God,
  It will flame out, like shining from shook foil;
  It gathers to a greatness, like the ooze of oil
Crushed. Why do men then now not reck his rod?
Generations have trod, have trod, have trod;
  And all is seared with trade; bleared, smeared with toil;
  And wears man's smudge and shares man's smell: the soil
Is bare now, nor can foot feel, being shod.

And for all this, nature is never spent;
  There lives the dearest freshness deep down things;
And though the last lights off the black West went
  Oh, morning, at the brown brink eastward, springs—
Because the Holy Ghost over the bent
  World broods with warm breast and with ah! bright wings.

Gerard Manley Hopkins
1844 - 1889

THE WORLD IS TOO MUCH WITH US

The world is too much with us; late and soon,
    Getting and spending, we lay waste our powers;
    Little we see in Nature that is ours;
We have given our hearts away, a sordid boon!
This Sea that bares her bosom to the moon,
    The winds that will be howling at all hours,
    And are up-gathered now like sleeping flowers,
For this, for everything, we are out of tune;
It moves us not. — Great God! I'd rather be
    A pagan suckled in a creed outworn;
So might I, standing on this pleasant lea,
    Have glimpses that would make me less forlorn;
Have sight of Proteus rising from the sea;
    Or hear old Triton blow his wreathed horn.

William Wordsworth
1770 - 1850

A FAINT JINGLE FROM THE UNIVERSE

There are many who are better
There are many who are worse
Those who write poems
And those who write verse
But even the Shakespeares, the Picassos, the Bachs
Were only arrangements of electrons and quarks.
Each of them could only follow the way
Dictated by Fate, their unique DNA.
So the simplest solution to set yourself free
Is to climb your own spiral and let yourself be.
What an unlikely mathematical chance

Created your life and led you this dance.
If you look at the galaxies above you at night
You may not be Einstein, but think how you might
Not have existed. How lucky you are
To live on your own particular star.
You'll waste precious time if all you do
Is envy the others who are different to you.
So if you don't want to end up the creek
You will have to accept that you are unique.
So consider the stars, the earth and the seas,
For such evolution should put you at ease.
Sweet is the dawn when the moon says good-bye
For yet one more day to the sun in the sky.
Yours is the Joy to use while you can
The instant of life that is yours as a man.

Peter Perrin
1917 -

THERE'S A CERTAIN SLANT OF LIGHT

There's a certain slant of light,
  On winter afternoons,
That oppresses, like the weight
  Of cathedral tunes.

Heavenly hurt, it gives us;
  We can find no scar,
But internal difference,
  Where the meanings are.

None may teach it anything,
  'T is the seal, despair;
An imperial affliction
  Sent us of the air.

136

When it comes, the landscape listens,
    Shadows hold their breath;
When it goes, 't is like the distance
    On the look of death.

Emily Dickinson
1830 - 1886

THERE IS A LADY SWEET AND KIND, Excerpt

There is a lady sweet and kind,
Was never face so pleased my mind.
    I did but see her passing by,
    And yet I love her till I die.

Her gesture, motion, and her smiles,
Her wit, her voice my heart beguiles,
    Beguiles my heart, I know not why,
    And yet I love her till I die.

Cupid is wing'ed and doth range,
Her country so my love doth change;
    But change the earth, or change the sky,
    Yet will I love her till I die.

Thomas Ford
c.1580 -1648

JOINING THE COLOURS
(West Kents, Dublin, 1914)

There they go marching all in step so gay!
    Smooth-cheeked and golden, food for shells and guns.
Blithely they go as to a wedding day,
    The mothers' sons.

The drab street stares to see them row on row
    On the high tram-tops, singing like the lark.
Too careless-gay for courage, singing they go
    Into the dark.

With tin whistles, mouth-organs, any noise,
    They pipe the way to glory and the grave;
Foolish and young, the gay and golden boys
    Love cannot save.

High heart! High courage! The poor girls they kissed
    Run with them: they shall kiss no more, alas!
Out of the mist they stepped – into the mist
    Singing they pass.

Katherine Tynan
1861 - 1931

JIM WHO RAN AWAY FROM HIS NURSE AND WAS EATEN BY A LION

There was a boy whose name was Jim;
His friends were very good to him.
They gave him tea, and cakes, and jam,
And slices of delicious ham,
And chocolate with pink inside,
And little tricycles to ride,
And read him stories through and through,
And even took him to the Zoo —
But there it was the dreadful fate
Befell him, which I now relate.

138

You know — at least you *ought* to know,
For I have often told you so —
That children never are allowed
To leave their nurses in a crowd;
Now this was Jim's especial foible,
He ran away when he was able,
And on this inauspicious day
He slipped his hand and ran away!
He hadn't gone a yard when — Bang!
With open jaws, a lion sprang,
And hungrily began to eat
The boy: beginning at his feet.

Now, just imagine how it feels
When first your toes and then your heels,
And then by gradual degrees,
Your shins and ankles, calves and knees,
Are slowly eaten, bit by bit.
No wonder Jim detested it!
No wonder that he shouted 'Hi!'
The honest keeper heard his cry,
Though very fat he almost ran
To help the little gentleman.
'Ponto!' he ordered as he came
(For Ponto was the lion's name),
'Ponto!' he cried, with angry frown
'Let go, Sir! Down, Sir! Put it down!'

The lion made a sudden stop,
He let the dainty morsel drop,
And slunk reluctant to his cage,
Snarling with disappointed rage.
But when he bent him over Jim,
The honest keeper's eyes were dim.
The lion having reached his head,
The miserable boy was dead!

When Nurse informed his parents, they
Were more concerned than I can say —
His Mother, as she dried her eyes,
Said, 'Well – it gives me no surprise,
He would not do as he was told!'
His Father, who was self-controlled,
Bade all the children round attend
To James's miserable end,
And always keep a-hold of Nurse
For fear of finding something worse.

Hilaire Belloc
1870 - 1953

INTIMATIONS OF IMMORTALITY, Excerpt One

There was a time when meadow, grove, and stream,
      The earth, and every common sight
      To me did seem
      Apparell'd in celestial light,
The glory and the freshness of a dream.
It is not now as it has been of yore;--
      Turn wheresoe'er I may,
      By night or day,
The things which I have seen I now can see no more!
      The rainbow comes and goes,
      And lovely is the rose;
      The moon doth with delight
Look round her when the heavens are bare;
      Waters on a starry night
      Are beautiful and fair;
The sunshine is a glorious birth;
But yet I know, where'er I go,
That there hath pass'd away a glory from the earth.

William Wordsworth
1770 - 1850

VITAE SUMMA BREVIS SPEM NOS VETAT INCOHARE LONGAM

They are not long, the weeping and the laughter,
Love and desire and hate;
I think they have no portion in us after
We pass the gate.

They are not long, the days of wine and roses.
Out of a misty dream
Our path emerges for a while, then closes
Within a dream.

Ernest Dowson
1867 - 1900

THE WAY THROUGH THE WOODS

They shut the road through the woods
Seventy years ago.
Weather and rain have undone it again,
And now you would never know
There was once a road through the woods
Before they planted the trees.
It is underneath the coppice and heath,
And the thin anemones.
Only the keeper sees
That, where the ring-dove broods,
And the badgers roll at ease,
There was once a road through the woods.

Yet, if you enter the woods
Of a summer evening late,
When the night-air cools on the trout-ringed pools
Where the otter whistles his mate,
(They fear not men in the woods,
Because they see so few)
You will hear the beat of a horse's feet
And the swish of a skirt in the dew,
Steadily cantering through
The misty solitudes,
As though they perfectly knew
The old lost road through the woods ....
But there is no road through the woods.

Rudyard Kipling
1865 - 1936

KING RICHARD THE SECOND, Excerpt
Act II, Scene I

Gaunt:

This royal throne of kings, this sceptered isle,
This earth of majesty, this seat of Mars,
This other Eden, demi-Paradise;
This fortress built by Nature for herself
Against infection and the hand of war;
This happy breed of men, this little world;
This precious stone set in the silver sea,
Which serves it in the office of a wall,
Or as a moat defensive to a house,
Against the envy of less happier lands;
This blessed plot, this earth, this realm, this England,
This nurse, this teeming womb of royal kings,
Fear'd by their breed, and famous by their birth,
Renowned for their deeds as far from home,
For Christian service and true chivalry,

142

As is the sepulchre, in stubborn Jewry,
Of the world's ransom, blessed Mary's Son;
This land of such dear souls, this dear dear land,
Dear for her reputation through the world,
Is now leas'd out – I die pronouncing it –
Like to a tenement or pelting farm:
England, bound in with the triumphant sea,
Whose rocky shore beats back the envious siege
Of watery Neptune, is now bound in with shame,
With inky blots, and rotten parchment bonds:
That England, that was wont to conquer others,
Hath made a shameful conquest of itself.
Ah, would the scandal vanish with my life,
How happy then were my ensuing death!

William Shakespeare
1564 - 1616

SONNET 2

Time does not bring relief; you all have lied
Who told me time would ease me of my pain!
I miss him in the weeping of the rain;
I want him at the shrinking of the tide;
The old snows melt from every mountain-side,
And last year's leaves are smoke in every lane;
But last year's bitter loving must remain
Heaped on my heart, and my old thoughts abide.
There are a hundred places where I fear
To go, - so with his memory they brim.
And entering with relief some quiet place
Where never fell his foot or shone his face
I say "There is no memory of him here!"
And so stand stricken, so remembering him.

Edna St Vincent Millay
1892 - 1950

AUGURIES OF INNOCENCE, Excerpt

To see a World in a Grain of Sand,
    And a Heaven in a Wild Flower,
Hold Infinity in the palm of your hand,
    And Eternity in an hour.

A Robin Redbreast in a Cage
Puts all Heaven in a Rage,
A dove-house filled with doves and Pigeons
Shudders Hell thro' all its regions.
A dog starv'd at his Master's Gate
Predicts the ruin of the State.
A Horse misus'd upon the Road
Calls to Heaven for Human blood.
Each outcry of the hunted Hare
A fibre from the Brain does tear.
A Skylark wounded in the wing,
A Cherubim does cease to sing.

William Blake
1757 - 1827

LESSONS OF THE WAR, Excerpt
To Alan Mitchell
Vixi duellis nuper idoneus
Et militavi non sine gloria

Naming of Parts

Today we have naming of parts. Yesterday,
We had daily cleaning. And tomorrow morning,
We shall have what to do after firing. But today,
Today we have naming of parts. Japonica
Glistens like coral in all of the neighbouring gardens,
    And today we have naming of parts.

144

This is the lower sling swivel. And this
Is the upper sling swivel, whose use you will see,
When you are given your slings. And this is the piling swivel,
Which in your case you have not got. The branches
Hold in the gardens their silent, eloquent gestures,
      Which in our case we have not got.

This is the safety-catch, which is always released
With an easy flick of the thumb. And please do not let me
See anyone using his finger. You can do it quite easy
If you have any strength in your thumb. The blossoms
Are fragile and motionless, never letting anyone see
      Any of them using their finger.

And this you can see is the bolt. The purpose of this
Is to open the breech, as you see. We can slide it
Rapidly backwards and forwards: we call this
Easing the spring. And rapidly backwards and forwards
The early bees are assaulting and fumbling the flowers:
      They call it easing the Spring.

They call it easing the Spring: it is perfectly easy
If you have any strength in your thumb: like the bolt,
And the breech, and the cocking-piece, and the point of
                              balance,
Which in our case we have not got; and the almond-blossom
Silent in all of the gardens, and the bees going backwards and
forwards,
      For today we have naming of parts.

Henry Reed
1914 - 1986

SPRING

To what purpose, April, do you return again?
Beauty is not enough.
You can no longer quiet me with the redness
Of little leaves opening stickily.
I know what I know.
The sun is hot on my neck as I observe
The spikes of the crocus.
The smell of the earth is good.
It is apparent that there is no death.
But what does that signify?
Not only underground are the brains of men
Eaten by maggots.
Life in itself
Is nothing,
An empty cup, a flight of uncarpeted stairs.
It is not enough that yearly, down this hill,
April
Comes like an idiot, babbling and strewing flowers.

Edna St Vincent Millay
1892 - 1950

JABBERWOCKY, from *Through the Looking-Glass*

'Twas brillig, and the slithy toves
   Did gyre and gimble in the wabe:
All mimsy were the borogoves
     And the mome raths outgrabe.

"Beware the Jabberwock, my son!
   The jaws that bite, the claws that catch!
Beware the Jubjub bird, and shun
     The frumious Bandersnatch!"

146

He took his vorpal sword in hand;
    Long time the manxome foe he sought—
So rested he by the Tumtum tree,
    And stood awhile in thought.

And, as in uffish thought he stood,
    The Jabberwock, with eyes of flame,
Came whiffling through the tulgey wood,
    And burbled as it came!

One, two! One, two! And through and through
    The vorpal blade went snicker-snack!
He left it dead, and with its head
    He went galumphing back.

"And hast thou slain the Jabberwock?
    Come to my arms, my beamish boy!
O frabjous day! Callooh, Callay!"
    He chortled in his joy.

'Twas brillig, and the slithy toves
    Did gyre and gimble in the wabe:
All mimsy were the borogoves,
    And the mome raths outgrabe.

Lewis Carroll
1832 - 1898

THE ROAD NOT TAKEN

Two roads diverged in a yellow wood,
And sorry I could not travel both
And be one traveller, long I stood
And looked down one as far as I could
To where it bent in the undergrowth;

Then took the other, as just as fair,
And having perhaps the better claim,
Because it was grassy and wanted wear;
Though as for that, the passing there
Had worn them really about the same,

And both that morning equally lay
In leaves no step had trodden black.
Oh, I kept the first for another day!
Yet knowing how way leads on to way,
I doubted if I should ever come back.

I shall be telling this with a sigh
Somewhere ages and ages hence:
Two roads diverged in a wood, and I –
I took the one less travelled by,
And that has made all the difference.

Robert Frost
1874 - 1963

GROWN-UP

Was it for this I uttered prayers,
And sobbed and cursed and kicked the stairs,
That now, domestic as a plate,
I should retire at half past eight?

Edna St Vincent Millay
1892 - 1950

148

ODE

We are the music-makers,
    And we are the dreamers of dreams,
Wandering by lone sea-breakers,
    And sitting by desolate streams;
World-losers and world-forsakers,
    On whom the pale moon gleams:
Yet we are the movers and shakers
    Of the world for ever, it seems.

With wonderful deathless ditties
We build up the world's great cities.
    And out of a fabulous story
    We fashion an empire's glory:
One man with a dream, at pleasure,
    Shall go forth and conquer a crown;
And three with a new song's measure
    Can trample an empire down.

We, in the ages lying
    In the buried past of the earth,
Built Nineveh with our sighing,
    And Babel itself with our mirth;
And o'erthrew them with prophesying
    To the old of the new world's worth;
For each age is a dream that is dying,
    Or one that is coming to birth.

Arthur O'Shaughnessy
1844 - 1881

FAREWELL TO A COLLEAGUE

We shall miss that Churchillian brow,
That subtle, erudite mind.
We shall have to be on our toes now
Or we'll find ourselves lagging behind.

He was our colleague in MI5,
Mainly deciphering Arabic prose;
He often appeared more dead than alive
Slumped in his chair in a doze.

If we never espy him again
We shall remember that resolute look
As he eases the cork from a bottle of champagne
And beams happily at the effort it took...

But we still feel his presence here
And often receive quite a fright
When glancing instinctively at his old chair
To regret it's a trick of the light.

Michael Baddeley
(in Memory of his old friend John Creighton)
Circa 2000

THE SONG OF THE UNGIRT RUNNERS

We swing ungirded hips,
And lighten'd are our eyes,
The rain is on our lips,
We do not run for prize.

We know not whom we trust
Nor witherward we fare,
But we run because we must
Through the great wide air.

The waters of the seas
Are troubled as by storm.
The tempest strips the trees
And does not leave them warm.

Does the tearing tempest pause?
Do the tree-tops ask it why?
So we run without a cause
'Neath the big bare sky.

The rain is on our lips,
We do not run for prize.
But the storm the water whips
And the wave howls to the skies.

The winds arise and strike it
And scatter it like sand,
And we run because we like it
Through the broad bright land.

Charles Hamilton Sorley
1895 - 1915

WERE A STAR

Were a star quenched on high,
    For ages would its light
Still travelling downwards from the sky
    Shine on our mortal night.
So, when a good man dies
    For years beyond our ken
The light he leaves behind him
    Shines upon the paths of men.

Anon
20th Century

WESTERN WIND

Western wind, when wilt thou blow,
The small rain down can rain?
Christ, if my love were in my arms
And I in my bed again!

Anon
16th Century

FORSAKING ALL OTHERS, Excerpt

What can you do with a woman's things
          After a woman is dead?
Not the bracelets and rings and strings
Of pearls, but the small unvalued things—
          What can I do, Wayne said.

What can you do with a woman's dresses,
          After a woman is dead?
Hanging limp in the cedar presses,
They are part of herself, her pretty dresses—
          What can I do, Wayne said.

What can you do with a woman's shoes,
          After a woman is dead?
Shoes that perhaps you helped her choose,
Poor little empty half-worn shoes—
          What can I do, Wayne said.

What can you do with her brush and comb,
          After a woman is dead?
What in God's name can you do with her home
And her loss and her love and her brush and comb—
          What can I do, Wayne said.

Alice Duer Miller
1874 - 1942

HARP SONG OF THE DANE WOMEN

What is a woman that you forsake her,
And the hearth-fire and the home-acre,
To go with the old grey Widow-maker?

She has no house to lay a guest in—
But one chill bed for all to rest in,
That the pale suns and the stray bergs nest in.

She has no strong white arms to fold you,
But the ten-times-fingering weed to hold you—
Out on the rocks where the tide has rolled you.

Yet, when the signs of summer thicken,
And the ice breaks, and the birch-buds quicken,
Yearly you turn from our side, and sicken—

Sicken again for the shouts and the slaughters.
You steal away to the lapping waters,
And look at your ship in her winter-quarters.

You forget our mirth, and talk at the tables,
The kine in the shed and the horse in the stables—
To pitch her sides and go over her cables.

Then you drive out where the storm-clouds swallow,
And the sound of your oar-blades, falling hollow,
Is all we have left through the months to follow.

Ah, what is Woman that you forsake her,
And the hearth-fire and the home-acre,
To go with the old grey Widow-maker?

Rudyard Kipling
1865 - 1936

LEISURE

What is this life if, full of care,
We have no time to stand and stare?

No time to stand beneath the boughs
And stare as long as sheep or cows.

No time to see, when woods we pass,
Where squirrels hide their nuts in grass.

No time to see, in broad daylight,
Streams full of stars, like skies at night.

No time to turn at Beauty's glance,
And watch her feet, how they can dance.

No time to wait till her mouth can
Enrich that smile her eyes began.

A poor life this if, full of care,
We have no time to stand and stare.

W.H. Davies
1871 - 1940

SONNET 42

What lips my lips have kissed, and where, and why,
I have forgotten, and what arms have lain
Under my head till morning; but the rain
Is full of ghosts tonight, that tap and sigh
Upon the glass and listen for reply,
And in my heart there stirs a quiet pain
For unremembered lads that not again
Will turn to me at midnight with a cry.
Thus in the winter stands the lonely tree,
Nor knows what birds have vanished one by one,
Yet knows its boughs more silent than before:
I cannot say what loves have come and gone,
I only know that summer sang in me
A little while, that in me sings no more.

Edna St Vincent Millay
1892 - 1950

ANTHEM FOR DOOMED YOUTH

What passing-bells for these who die as cattle?
Only the monstrous anger of the guns.
Only the stuttering rifles' rapid rattle
Can patter out their hasty orisons.
No mockeries for them; no prayers nor bells,
Nor any voice of mourning save the choirs, —
The shrill, demented choirs of wailing shells;
And bugles calling for them from sad shires.

What candles may be held to speed them all?
Not in the hands of boys, but in their eyes
Shall shine the holy glimmers of good-byes.
The pallor of girls' brows shall be their pall;
Their flowers the tenderness of patient minds,
And each slow dusk a drawing-down of blinds.

Wilfred Owen
1893 - 1918

THOUGHTS IN A GARDEN, Excerpt

What wondrous life is this I lead!
Ripe apples drop about my head;
The luscious clusters of the vine
Upon my mouth do crush their wine;
The nectarine and curious peach
Into my hands themselves do reach;
Stumbling on melons, as I pass,
Ensnared with flowers, I fall on grass.

Meanwhile the mind from pleasure less
Withdraws into its happiness;
The mind, that Ocean where each kind
Does straight its own resemblance find;
Yet it creates, transcending these,
Far other worlds, and other seas;
Annihilating all that's made
To a green thought in a green shade.

Andrew Marvell
1621 - 1678

THE DONKEY

When fishes flew and forests walked,
    And figs grew upon thorn,
Some moment when the moon was blood
    Then surely I was born;

With monstrous head and sickening cry
    And ears like errant wings,
The devil's walking parody
    On all four-footed things.

The tattered outlaw of the earth,
    Of ancient crooked will —
Starve, scourge, deride me: I am dumb,
    I keep my secret still.

Fools! For I also had my hour;
    One far fierce hour and sweet;
There was a shout about my ears,
    And palms before my feet.

G.K. Chesterton
1874 - 1936

SONG

When I am dead, my dearest,
    Sing no sad songs for me;
Plant thou no roses at my head,
    Nor shady cypress tree:

Be the green grass above me
    With showers and dewdrops wet;
And if thou wilt, remember,
    And if thou wilt, forget.

I shall not see the shadows,
    I shall not feel the rain;
I shall not hear the nightingale
    Sing on, as if in pain:

And dreaming through the twilight
    That doth not rise nor set,
Haply I may remember,
    And haply may forget.

Christina Rossetti
1830 - 1894

SONNET 19
On His Blindness

When I consider how my light is spent,
E're half my days in this dark world and wide,
And that one Talent which is death to hide,
Lodg'd with me useless, though my Soul more bent
To serve therewith my Maker, and present
My true account, lest He returning chide;
'Doth God exact day-labour, light deny'd?'
I fondly ask ; But Patience, to prevent
That murmur, soon replies, 'God doth not need
Either man's work or his own gifts. Who best
Bear his mild yoke, they serve him best, his State
Is Kingly. Thousands at his bidding speed,
And post o'er Land and Ocean without rest:
They also serve who only stand and wait.'

John Milton
1608 - 1674

SAM

When Sam goes back in memory,
It is to where the sea
Breaks on the shingle, emerald-green,
In white foam, endlessly;
He says – with small brown eyes on mine –
"I used to keep awake,
And lean from my window in the moon,
Watching those billows break.
And half a million tiny hands,
And eyes, like sparks of frost,
Would dance and come tumbling into the moon,
On every breaker tossed.
And all across from star to star,
I've seen the watery sea,

160

With not a single ship in sight,
Just ocean there, and me;
And heard my father snore. And once,

As sure as I'm alive,
Out of those wallowing, moon-flecked waves
I saw a mermaid dive;
Head and shoulders above the wave,
Plain as I now see you,
Combing her hair, now back, now front,

Her two eyes peeping through;
Calling me "Sam!" – quietlike – "Sam!"….
But me ….. I never went,
Making believe I kind of thought
'Twas some one else she meant ….
Wonderful lovely there she sat,
Singing the night away,
All in the solitudinous sea
Of that there lonely bay."
"P'raps," and he'd smooth his hairless mouth,
"P'raps if 'twere now, my son,
P'raps, if I heard a voice say, 'Sam!'….
Morning would find me gone."

Walter de la Mare
1873 - 1956

NORTH - WEST PASSAGE

1. GOOD NIGHT

When the bright lamp is carried in,
The sunless hours again begin;
O'er all without, in field and lane,
The haunted night returns again.

Now we behold the embers flee
About the firelit hearth; and see
Our faces painted as we pass,
Like pictures, on the window-glass.

Must we to bed indeed? Well then,
Let us arise and go like men,
And face with an undaunted tread
The long black passage up to bed.

Farewell, O brother, sister, sire!
O pleasant party round the fire!
The songs you sing, the tales you tell,
Till far tomorrow, fare ye well!

2. SHADOW MARCH

All round the house is the jet-black night;
It stares through the window-pane;
It crawls in the corners, hiding from the light,
And it moves with the moving flame.

Now my little heart goes a-beating like a drum,
With the breath of the Bogie in my hair;
And all round the candle the crooked shadows come
And go marching along up the stair.

The shadows of the balusters, the shadow of the lamp,
The shadow of the child that goes to bed -
All the wicked shadows coming, tramp, tramp, tramp,
With the black night overhead.

3. IN PORT

Last to the chamber where I lie
My fearful footsteps patter nigh,
And come from out the cold and gloom
Into my warm and cheerful room.

There, safe arrived, we turn about
To keep the coming shadows out,
And close the happy door at last
On all the perils that we passed.

Then, when mamma goes by to bed,
She shall come in with tip-toe tread,
And see me lying warm and fast
And in the Land of Nod at last.

Robert Louis Stevenson
1850 - 1894

WHEN YOU ARE OLD

When you are old and grey and full of sleep,
And nodding by the fire, take down this book,
And slowly read, and dream of the soft look
Your eyes had once, and of their shadows deep;

How many loved your moments of glad grace,
And loved your beauty with love false or true;
But one man loved the pilgrim soul in you,
And loved the sorrows of your changing face.

164

And bending down beside the glowing bars
Murmur, a little sadly, how love fled
And paced upon the mountains overhead
And hid his face amid a crowd of stars.

William Butler Yeats
1865 - 1939

LINES AND SQUARES

Whenever I walk in a London street,
I'm ever so careful to watch my feet;
And I keep in the squares,
And the masses of bears,
Who wait at the corners all ready to eat
The sillies who tread on the lines of the street,
Go back to their lairs,
And I say to them, "Bears,
Just look how I'm walking in all the squares!"

And the little bears growl to each other, "He's mine,
As soon as he's silly and steps on a line."
And some of the bigger bears try to pretend
That they came round the corner to look for a friend;
And they try to pretend that nobody cares
Whether you walk on the lines or squares.

But only the sillies believe their talk;
It's ever so portant how you walk.
And it's ever so jolly to call out, "Bears,
Just watch me walking in all the squares!"

A.A. Milne
1882 - 1956

166

THE STOLEN CHILD

Where dips the rocky highland
Of Sleuth Wood in the lake,
There lies a leafy island
Where flapping herons wake
The drowsy water-rats;
There we've hid our faery vats
Full of berries,
And of reddest stolen cherries.
Come away, O human child!
To the waters and the wild
With a faery, hand in hand,
For the world's more full of weeping than you can understand.

Where the wave of moonlight glosses
The dim grey sands with light,
Far off by furthest Rosses
We foot it all the night.
Weaving olden dances,
Mingling hands and mingling glances
Till the moon has taken flight;
To and fro we leap
And chase the frothy bubbles,
While the world is full of troubles
And is anxious in its sleep.
Come away, O human child!
To the waters and the wild
With a faery hand in hand
For the world's more full of weeping than you can understand.

Where the wandering water gushes
From the hills above Glen-Car,
In pools among the rushes
That scarce could bathe a star,
We seek for slumbering trout
And whispering in their ears
Give them unquiet dreams;
Leaning softly out
From ferns that drop their tears

Over the young streams.
Come away, O human child,
To the waters and the wild
With a faery, hand in hand,
For the world's more full of weeping than you can understand.

Away with us he's going,
The solemn eyed:
He'll hear no more the lowing
Of the calves on the warm hillside
Or the kettle on the hob
Sing peace into his breast,
Or see the brown mice bob
Round and round the oatmeal chest.
For he comes, the human child!
To the waters and the wild
With a faery, hand in hand,
For the world's more full of weeping than he can understand.

W.B. Yeats
1865 - 1939

BOY ON THE GATE

Where the hedge spread wide
He climbed the gate
Which, wired and stapled,
Green with age,
Stood unopened all the years I knew.
Its cobwebbed corners, in the mornings
Hung with dew.

On one side a field grew lush
And on the other
Brambles reached and clung
Across a steep banked brook.
Rotted and time abused,
A broken bridge spanned swirling depths,
And so the gate became unused.

Convolvulus in china white,
Bryony and honeysuckle intertwined.
Snarling, gruff among worn stones,
Deep down the brook rushed on
To lower meads.
Its treachery hidden beneath
The growth of hedge and weeds.

In fear of depth,
Yet placing feet so near the edge,
The boy leaned further from the gate
To pick blackberries.
Scratched hands, scratched face,
He loved the danger
Of this place.

Jennie Horsman
1937 -

VALIANT-FOR-TRUTH'S SONG

Who would true Valour see
Let him come hither;
One here will Constant be,
Come Wind, come Weather.
There's no Discouragement
Shall make him once Relent,
His first avow'd Intent,
To be a Pilgrim.

Who so beset him round,
With dismal Stories,
Do but themselves Confound;
His Strength the more is.
No Lyon can him fright,
He'll with a Giant Fight,
But he will have a right,
To be a Pilgrim.

Hobgoblin, nor foul Fiend,
Can daunt his Spirit;
He knows, he at the end,
Shall Life Inherit.
Then Fancies fly away,
He'll fear not what men say,
He'll labour Night and Day,
To be a Pilgrim.

John Bunyan
1628 - 1688

STOPPING BY WOODS ON A SNOWY EVENING

Whose woods these are I think I know.
His house is in the village, though;
He will not see me stopping here
To watch his woods fill up with snow.

My little horse must think it queer
To stop without a farmhouse near
Between the woods and frozen lake
The darkest evening of the year.

He gives his harness bells a shake
To ask if there is some mistake.
The only other sound's the sweep
Of easy wind and downy flake.

The woods are lovely, dark and deep.
But I have promises to keep,
And miles to go before I sleep.
And miles to go before I sleep.

Robert Frost
1874 - 1963

VIA NEGATIVA

Why not! I never thought other than
That God is that great absence
In our lives, the empty silence
Within, the place where we go
Seeking, not in hope to
Arrive or find. He keeps the interstices
In our knowledge, the darkness
Between stars. His are the echoes
We follow, the footprints he has just
Left. We put our hands in
His side hoping to find
It warm. We look at people
And places as though he had looked
At them, too; but miss the reflection.

R.S. Thomas
1913 - 2000

THE SHEPHERD

With every new born lamb
I see his hands,
Gnarled, weathered,
Yet so able to deliver
That yellow squirming mass
Of unfolding anxious limbs.

In every smothered bleat
Uttered by those mothering
Their freshly suckled young,
I hear his voice,
Gruff, confident and hushed,
Words for sheep alone.

On every bud-burnt night
I hear his tread,
The rasp of boots on frozen grass,
And see those misty mounds
He tends
Where the land lies sheltered.

With every flower and frond
I lay upon this marble,
I see a man
Who cleaves the burrs and briars
And tells of warmth and calm
In Spring to come.

Jennie Horsman
1937 -

HE FELL AMONG THIEVES

"Ye have robb'd," said he, "ye have slaughter'd and made an end,
Take your ill-got plunder, and bury the dead:
What will ye more of your guest and sometime friend?"
    "Blood for our blood," they said.

He laugh'd: "If one may settle the score for five,
I am ready; but let the reckoning stand till day:
I have loved the sunlight as dearly as any alive."
    "You shall die at dawn," said they.

He flung his empty revolver down the slope,
He climb'd alone to the Eastward edge of the trees;
All night long in a dream untroubled of hope
    He brooded, clasping his knees.

He did not hear the monotonous roar that fills
The ravine where the Yassin river sullenly flows;
He did not see the starlight on the Laspur hills,
    Or the far Afghan snows.

He saw the April noon on his books aglow,
The wisteria trailing in at the window wide;
He heard his father's voice from the terrace below
    Calling him down to ride.

He saw the grey little church across the park,
The mounds that hid the loved and honour'd dead;
The Norman arch, the chancel softly dark,
    The brasses black and red.

He saw the School Close, sunny and green,
The runner beside him, the stand by the parapet wall,
The distant tape, and the crowd roaring between,
    His own name over all.

He saw the dark wainscot and timber'd roof,
The long tables, and the faces merry and keen;
The College Eight and their trainer dining aloof,
    The Dons on the dais serene.

He watch'd the liner's stem ploughing the foam,
He felt her trembling speed and the thrash of her screw;
He heard the passengers' voices talking of home,
    He saw the flag she flew.

And now it was dawn. He rose strong on his feet,
And strode to his ruin'd camp below the wood;
He drank the breath of the morning cool and sweet:
    His murderers round him stood.

Light on the Laspur hills was broadening fast,
The blood-red snow-peaks chill'd to a dazzling white;
He turn'd, and saw the golden circle at last,
    Cut by the Eastern height.

"O glorious Life, Who dwellest in earth and sun,
I have lived, I praise and adore Thee." A sword swept.
Over the pass the voices one by one
    Faded, and the hill slept.

Sir Henry Newbolt
1862 - 1938

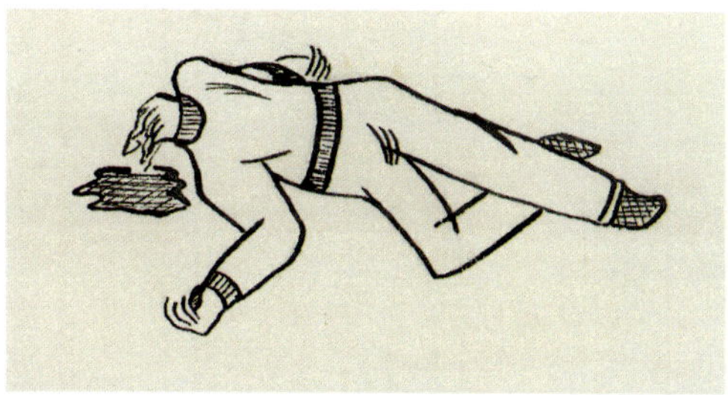

ADLESTROP

Yes, I remember Adlestrop—
The name, because one afternoon
Of heat the express-train drew up there
Unwontedly. It was late June.

The steam hissed. Someone cleared his throat;
No one left and no one came
On the bare platform. What I saw
Was Adlestrop—only the name

And willows, willow-herb and grass,
And meadowsweet, and haycocks dry;
No whit less still and lonely fair
Than the high cloudlets in the sky.

And for that minute a blackbird sang
Close by, and round him, mistier,
Farther and farther, all the birds
Of Oxfordshire and Gloucestershire.

Edward Thomas
1878 - 1917

DECLENSION

You are the ablative of my existence, I thought
And wondered, that such a word
Should so present itself,
Years from the Latin class.
"By, with or from a thing"
That's ablative, the all-embracing.
Genitive, the pinched, holds "of",
Dative has merely "to",
But ablative with splendour bursts —
"By, with or from a thing".
By you is life turned on each day,
My world illuminated.
With you, my love, are days transformed
And suddenly made dear.
From you springs happiness and peace and joy.
Funny old Romans, marshalling their words like armies,
Each soldier firmly in his place.
Funny little schoolgirl, cross and pig-tailed
Scowling and scribbling in her Latin Grammar.
But, oh, they knew what they were at,
Those ancient Empire builders.
And, child, admit that you were wrong,
Grumbling about a language dead and wasted youth.
Where would you be today without a word to fit your lover?
Glorious ablative is there to put him in his place.

Sally Cade
1935 -

THE LESSON

'Your father's gone', my bald headmaster said.
His shiny dome and brown tobacco jar
Splintered at once in tears. It wasn't grief.
I cried for knowledge which was bitterer
Than any grief. For there and then I knew
That grief has uses – that a father dead
Could bind the bully's fist a week or two;
And then I cried for shame, then for relief.

I was a month past ten when I learnt this:
I still remember how the noise was stilled
In school-assembly when my grief came in.
Some goldfish in a bowl quietly sculled
Around their shining prison on its shelf.
They were indifferent. All the other eyes
Were turned towards me. Somewhere in myself
Pride, like a goldfish, flashed a sudden fin.

Edward Lucie-Smith
1933 -

AFTERWORDS...

SARAH'S ANTHOLOGY

You see yourself moving out
Of a photograph of your garden
Filled with dappled light and summer sun,
Captured by a lens forever.

You in turn see this as passing out
From the living heart of life,
Yet it is only an illusion: move
A camera to the left and lo!
You are back at the centre.

Each of us remains the focus
Of a sensory universe:
Only children and lovers
Can displace us for a time
To the edge of our own life.

One of the privileges of age
Is the chance to re-centre,
To create anthologies and artefacts
That give pleasure and solace to others,
Spreading way beyond any other photo,
To ripple out through lives and time.

Death is never the end,
Relationships, conversations go on,
Reminders and memories vibrate,
Like music composed of love
In acts of kindness.

Pablo Foster
1936 –
(Written February 2007)

First lines
TITLE
Author